ATYP's The Voices Project:
THE ENCORE EDITION

We Live in the City, Don't We? by Holly Brindley
Bitchin' Soul by Kirsty Budding
Food by Didem Caia
B-T-Dubs Mum… by Lucy Coleman
William Burroughs' Wife by Grace De Morgan
Rupture by Kendall Feaver
Boys Don't Believe in Fairies by Josh Forward
Meat by Sunday Emerson Gullifer
Anyu by Zsuzsanna Ihar
Soap by Ava Karuso
Penny Drops by Bianca Kostic-London
Cliffs of Mohr by Kate McDowell
A Language of Our Own by Faith Ng
The Panel by Lauren Sherritt
Old King Coal by Fregmonto Stokes
A Living Room by Jessica Tovey
Lesson 88 by Jessie Tu

CURRENCY PRESS
SYDNEY

Australian Theatre
for Young People

CURRENCY PLAYS

First published in 2015
by Currency Press Pty Ltd,
PO Box 2287, Strawberry Hills, NSW, 2012, Australia
enquiries@currency.com.au
www.currency.com.au

We Live in the City, Don't We? © Holly Brindley, 2015; *Bitchin' Soul* © Kirsty Budding, 2015; *Food* © Didem Caia, 2015; *B-T-Dubs Mum...* © Lucy Coleman, 2015; *William Burrough's Wife* © Grace De Morgan, 2015; *Rupture* © Kendall Feaver, 2015; *Boys Don't Believe in Fairies* © Josh Forward, 2015; *Meat* © Sunday Emerson Gullifer, 2015; *Anyu* © Zsuzsanna Ihar, 2015; *Soap* © Ava Karuso, 2015; *Penny Drops* © Bianca Kostic-London, 2015; *Cliffs of Mohr* © Kate McDowell, 2015; *A Language of Our Own* © Faith Ng, 2015; *The Panel* © Lauren Sherritt, 2015; *Old King Coal* © Fregmonto Stokes, 2015; *A Living Room* © Jessica Tovey, 2015; *Lesson 88* © Jessie Tu, 2015.

COPYING FOR EDUCATIONAL PURPOSES

The Australian *Copyright Act 1968* (Act) allows a maximum of one chapter or 10% of this book, whichever is the greater, to be copied by any educational institution for its educational purposes provided that that educational institution (or the body that administers it) has given a remuneration notice to Copyright Agency Limited (CAL) under the Act.

For details of the CAL licence for educational institutions contact CAL, Level 15, 233 Castlereagh Street, Sydney, NSW, 2000; tel: within Australia 1800 066 844 toll free; outside Australia 61 2 9394 7600; fax: 61 2 9394 7601; email: info@copyright.com.au

COPYING FOR OTHER PURPOSES

Except as permitted under the Act, for example a fair dealing for the purposes of study, research, criticism or review, no part of this book may be reproduced, stored in a retrieval system, or transmitted in any form or by any means without prior written permission. All enquiries should be made to the publisher at the address above.

Any performance or public reading of any play within this collection is forbidden unless a licence has been received from the author or the author's agent. The purchase of this book in no way gives the purchaser the right to perform any of these plays in public, whether by means of a staged production or a reading. All applications for public performance should be addressed to the author/s c/– Currency Press.

Cataloguing-in-publication data for this title is available from the National Library of Australia website: www.nla.gov.au

Typeset by Dean Nottle for Currency Press.
Cover design by Alissa Dinallo.

Currency Press acknowledges the Traditional Owners of the Country on which we live and work. We pay our respects to all Aboriginal and Torres Strait Islander Elders, past and present.

Contents

v   The Unpublished Collection: Introduction by Fraser Corfield

Encore Edition

- 1   *We Live in the City, Don't We?* by Holly Brindley
- 6   *Bitchin' Soul* by Kirsty Budding
- 10   *Food* by Didem Caia
- 14   *B-T-Dubs Mum…* by Lucy Coleman
- 20   *William Burroughs' Wife* by Grace De Morgan
- 25   *Rupture* by Kendall Feaver
- 30   *Boys Don't Believe in Fairies* by Josh Forward
- 35   *Meat* by Sunday Emerson Gullifer
- 44   *Anyu* by Zsuzsanna Ihar
- 54   *Soap* by Ava Karuso
- 60   *Penny Drops* by Bianca Kostic-London
- 64   *Cliffs of Mohr* by Kate McDowell
- 70   *A Language of Our Own* by Faith Ng
- 73   *The Panel* by Lauren Sherritt
- 78   *Old King Coal* by Fregmonto Stokes
- 82   *A Living Room* by Jessica Tovey
- 89   *Lesson 88* by Jessie Tu

We encourage anyone producing and casting this work to consider performers from diverse backgrounds.

THE UNPUBLISHED COLLECTION
Fraser Corfield

The monologues in this publication provide an outstanding resource for young adult actors looking for material written specifically for them. These pieces provide us with authentic young voices telling stories as diverse as the artists who wrote them. Funny, poignant, poetic and at times heartbreaking, these scripts reflect the transformative power of simple storytelling. Each piece has the potential to take its audience on an emotional journey seen through the eyes of a young Australian.

Since the first Voices Project was staged by ATYP in 2011 under the title *Tell It Like It Isn't*, this annual initiative has transformed the Australian theatrical landscape for young playwrights and actors. The scripts, published by Currency Press, have been performed across the country. Many of the playwrights who created them have gone on to work with our nation's leading professional theatre companies and are counted as rising stars of the industry. The monologues that have been made into short films have been seen by more than one million people around the world.

But the scripts published so far only represent half the story. Each year The National Studio involves twenty outstanding young writers aged between 18 and 26 who each create a seven minute monologue suitable for a 17-year-old actor. Sadly, only half of these can be presented as ATYP's first production of each year. It demands a lot of an audience to sit through seventy minutes of monologues in an evening, no matter how well they are written and performed. As a result, every year there are ten monologues that are not produced, and therefore don't get published

The selection process for The Voices Project is always arduous, always contentious. Like so many aspects of the performing arts there are times when the selection feels unjust, even when you are involved in the decision-making. Works are not programed on the basis of choosing 'the best', which of course is a completely subjective notion anyway. They have been curated each year to form a night of theatre. This has meant each year pieces could be overlooked because they were too similar, too different, couldn't be cast from the actors who auditioned or there were too many written for that gender that year. Something that was not performed or published one year might have been selected had it been in the mix the following year.

We are thrilled that Currency Press has curated this collection of previously unpublished pieces. Like the editions of The Voices Project before them, they deserve to be seen around the country. On behalf of all those that have been involved in The Voices Project – Lachlan Philpott who came up with the idea for an annual monologues program, Dan Pritchard who gave it its name, Jenni Medway who runs it today and the many outstanding playwrights and dramaturges who have been mentors and participants from around Australia – I offer our heartfelt congratulations to the playwrights presented.

Sydney
October 2015
Fraser Corfield
Artistic Director, ATYP

WE LIVE IN THE CITY, DON'T WE?
HOLLY BRINDLEY

Pause.

Sorry, fuck, fuck, that was a dickhead thing to do, to kiss your— instead of—

I didn't mean to kiss your head. You seem pissed off?

I wasn't sure what to do, I didn't mean to treat you like a little kid or—

I know it was really fucked up and rude when I said I wanted you to leave and go home, but, I didn't say that because I don't…

Pause.

The thing is, what I want to tell you is that—

You make me feel sick.

In a good way! Don't go inside yet, please.

It's because, okay—

Usually when I'm fucking someone I don't realize that I'm naked.

But when we fucked I *did* realize I was naked and it made me feel kind of sick. But also it made me more, sort of, it made me happy, as if all the other times I've fucked it wasn't *really* fucking. It was like *I* was fucking a thing, or, actually a *someone*, don't worry it *was* a *someone*. But it was just me. Not um, it wasn't me *with* someone else, being there together and…

THE VOICES PROJECT: ENCORE EDITION

Your skin was so warm which made me realize that *I* have skin. Cause unless it's really hot or really cold you don't usually notice that you *have* skin on your body and that it can *feel* things. But because *your* skin was so warm, it made me realize that *I* have skin.

And you have the shiniest hair, it's slippery and kind of a mirror, I'm, it's hard to look in your eyes and explain, but I want to, because—

I wish we could start this day over because—

If I let my mind think, if I let it go off on its own, then it won't ever *stop* thinking so I always do whatever I can to make sure that I'm never left alone with my thoughts. There's got to be noise all the time to drown everything else out, there's got to be noise or things to look at or things to do or someone to fuck and sometimes all that shit gets in the way of having a conversation with someone, of having a *real* conversation with *you*. I wanted you to go home so that we could start again because I think with *you* I might not mind so much if it's quiet, or—

I have to be drunk all the time. I like to be drunk so that all my conversations mean nothing but then I'm also scared of getting *too* drunk because then my conversations might mean *everything*. So I go away and there's... things. There's, see I want you to know that I'm... I go away, I walk down the street right to the end where there's a car park, do you know it? No, you don't know it, and so it's a car park but if you jump the fence into this one section of it there's a patch of grass which I love cause it's just this patch of grass in the middle of the concrete which is crazy, so when I sit on it, on the patch of grass, I feel like, I dunno, like I'm sitting on a magic carpet or something and I like to go there, it's a patch of grass. Nobody knows. And if I squint my eyes I can see a lake in the distance which is weird because... we live in the city, don't we? I just sit there and, just sit there to *be* there.

And I can watch the cars going past on the road nearby and the speed limit is sixty which isn't that fast but it's fast

We Live in the City, Don't We?

enough that it takes my mind away from my thoughts. There are heaps of things to watch and it's not far from that road that has all those hookers, where all the hookers work. So sometimes they wander back up past the car park and I can see them and they look, I don't know, like they're always cold. Even if it's a sunny day. Why don't they bring jumpers? And one time I thought about running over to one of them who was walking not far from me and she had her arms crossed and her head was down and she had the longest hair down to her waist and it was messy but it looked really clean and um, it was... so she seemed as if she might be cold and I thought about taking my jumper off and giving it to her. I'd take it off and say, 'Arms up' and she'd put her arms up and I'd slide my jumper over her hands, arms, head, chest, stomach and she'd be wearing my jumper and it would probably be too big for her.

Don't you think? Do *you* need somewhere to go? I mean, please *don't* go in, don't leave, I asked because I don't know if you're like me. I *think* you're like me, I *hope* you're like me, at least in *some* ways I do, in *some* ways I wouldn't wish that on you, because, anyway—

I go to the car park and there I am. But actually I'm not there, my mind is there, but look, my body isn't, my body isn't there on the grass, my body is not there on the grass. It's not. Because *I'm* not there because there's definitely no lake and maybe, probably, definitely, no patch of grass actually because why would there be a patch of grass in the middle of a car park next to an apartment block?

My point is, that I didn't mean to kiss you on the forehead as if you were my little sister or something, I was just trying to go back and start over, get to some clear place, something with—

I don't want to treat you like that, that's not what I think you are I don't think you're her, she's not even a her, there isn't a her, she's not you and you're not her. So why would I kiss you on the forehead? It's not because I didn't enjoy fucking you, not because I don't think you're sexy, but that's the whole thing, I wanted to kiss your mouth but I didn't want the mouth kiss to say anything that was too much.

I was aiming for your mouth but I connected with your head, and you have a nice, such a *nice* head and a great face and she's dead and you were standing right there and my brain was saying to me, 'Kiss her goodnight, kiss her goodnight, kiss her goodnight' but it was the *afternoon*. They always said 'Kiss your sister goodnight' but they don't know. I wanted to kiss you goodnight because I think she was dead after I kissed her goodnight with the pillow, five, goodnight with the pillow, when I was five, and you were right there for me to kiss *now*. And I thought of her, maybe because *your* eyes are so deep brown and *her* eyes were so deep brown like a cow's, that sounds like an insult but it's actually a compliment. I like cows, I think they're beautiful, no a *horse*, yeah a horse's eyes, with the longest eyelashes, I hope you don't mind, I'm sorry, I think, I think, I think it was me, I'm so nervous, but I can't quite remember and maybe I just made it up because of the car park and the grass. That's what makes me think that I'm not sure if I can remember it or if I've *made up* that I can remember it but either way she was a *warm* baby that became a *cold* one and it might've been the pillow that I might've put on her face for a goodnight kiss and the more I think about it the more I think that maybe you kind of look like *she* would have looked if she'd grown up except she didn't so I found a patch of grass and I love your um, your cunt except I kissed you on the forehead because I didn't want you to think that *that's* all it is for me and also your eyes look like a horse's eyes and *her* eyes looked like a horse's, or a foal's because she was a baby and *you* are not, trust me, I know that *you're not*, I didn't mean to treat you like a kid, but I was a kid, but your eyes and you have the shiniest hair, I'm repeating myself and I'm telling you all of the, things—

I'm sorry, the thing is, is that all I wanted to do was kiss your mouth again. But I ended up kissing your head because I just wanted to kiss you sweetly so that you would think *I'm* sweet. And nice. And someone you'd maybe want to go out with sometime. And we could go back to my house and it'd be different, just talking, and I'd walk you home again and stand

We Live in the City, Don't We?

here and ask you out on a date or something. Because I don't just want to fuck you. Because I don't. I don't just want to fuck you.

▼ ▼ ▼ ▼ ▼

BITCHIN' SOUL
KIRSTY BUDDING

Lights up on Jaslyn, 18, at a house party.

You know when someone insults you while they're pretending to be your best friend? Jessica starts conversationally bitch-slapping me and I can see it happening like that moment in *The Lion King* when Scar reaches out to pull Mufasa from the ledge, then digs in his claws.

And I'm like, 'Hey bitch, your blonde hair extensions can't hide your black soul. These people may think you're hot, but isn't it ironic that you love taking photos of yourself because you hate yourself? Looking through your Instagram is like x-raying the Mona Lisa and seeing The Scream.'

She doesn't get the art reference, like she doesn't get me. Good. Must mean I'm more complicated than a blow job.

She clacks away in her tacky shoes and I'm alone again, calm—like, I'm not touched by anyone because I've given up on people. I'm that girl at the house party who's in the house but outside the party, watching like a hawk. I say a hawk because they have amazing sight but also because they're above everyone else.

Down there, Jessica and her friends move in drunken formation. It's the social survival of the fittest; competitions include swearing, taking selfies, bitching about absent friends, and making the most frequent, slightly ironic use of the word 'bae'. Urgh.

I grab a drink and a guy starts talking to me. This always gets awkward.

'Hey, I just met you and this is crazy, but I can see your soul so I'm not attracted to you.'

Bitchin' Soul

He walks off staring at his arms and I'm like ha-ha… his self-esteem hurts.

Mum says I should stop being myself in public. Meh. I'll just stand near this group and fake-laugh while photobombing their Facebook pics looking bored and slightly repulsed.

Oh, look. Some guy is setting his arm hair on fire. Everyone seems really impressed. Now they're taking off their shirts and sculling drinks and lifting things… and asking each other if they even lift… bro… and then laughing…

Seriously, I'm like someone at a zoo searching for a laminated explanation of what the fuck I'm looking at.

They start doing a four-way push up. One guy rests his feet on another guy's shoulders, who rests his feet on another guy's shoulders, until the four of them lift as one, forming a seemingly macho but totally homoerotic square. I decide that what I'm seeing here—the extreme focus in their eyes and Jessica cheering like the earth is hanging in the balance of their biceps—this is the reason we haven't eradicated poverty in the third world.

People are so dumb. Not just young people, but like, all people. Not dumb intelligence-wise necessarily, just so… unaware of themselves. They zombie around buying shit they don't need to feed their hungry egos clawing at their caged lives, then they boast about the bars. Check out the bars on my cage, bro. They're brand-name bars. They're uni fees and a job and a mortgage and a pension and...

Mum says I think too much. Thinking too much is bad. If you're wise then you wish you weren't. Normal people are wary of me, like the antelope in *The Lion King*—fuck that's a great film—because I see them. I can read their faces better than they can read words but it's hurting my eyes and I have to get out.

She breathes in as she steps out into the night.

You know what I notice most, when I'm drunk? The feel of the air on my skin; how it feels cold in a different way—like being surrounded by something hard and black, but cold. The stars are cold too, and random, like our existence. It's weird how I can see everything but my eyes don't matter. I'm just alone and insignificant on some bitch's lawn.

And Mum's waiting in the car because I'm a loser.

She's like, 'Hi baby, how was the party? Did you and Jessica make friends?'

I'm like, 'No, Mum; Jessica's a whore.'

She's all like, 'Don't talk about your sister like that.'

Then Jessica gets in the car: 'Oh my god, Mum, can you not make me take that bitch to parties? It's, like, so embarrassing.'

'Hey Jessica? Your vagina smells like a bucket of semen. Because it is one.'

Mum tells me off. Bit unfair. Jessica didn't get anything for the bitch comment, which I feel was way below the belt.

So we're driving to McDonalds and Jessica's going on and on about what a bitch I am. All I did was tell everyone about her ugly soul. That's not a lie, unlike her face.

Then she starts crying.

You know what pisses me off about Jessica? It doesn't irritate me that she's weak. It irritates me that she pretends to be strong. I don't care if she hates herself. I care that her way of covering that up is to act like she loves herself.

And she's crying.

'Why should I feel bad? It's not pleasant, you know, being able to see souls. Like, I can see Mum's soul and it loves yours more than mine, and it… it misses Dad's more than anything since he left.'

Jessica's crying rather a lot now. Mum's gone quiet; all I can

Bitchin' Soul

see are her hands on the wheel.

'It's not my fault you've got a bitch-soul, OK! I'm sorry you hate yourself and that you're too dumb to work that out, but the truth is better than your Barbie extensions and fake eyelashes, which are coming unglued by the way, so just shut the fuck up!'

I've done it. I've brought up her soul and she vomits on the floor of the car.

It smells bad—really bad—as if the vomit is sad.

I'm not sure why my soul softens then. Maybe it's because I didn't hold back her hair and now her blonde extensions are brown… the colour her hair was when she was my little sister; or because she's looking into the pool of spew and realising she's not in love with her reflection. I kind of wish she could find that pool of water somewhere where she's beautiful at the bottom.

I'm also frustrated that the drive-through lady can't hear my order over all the crying and the spewing, so I look at Jessica and decide to wear my soul on my sleeve.

'Jessica, do you know why people are bitches? It's because they know, deep down, that they're a bitch, and that makes them hate themselves, so they have to bitch about someone else—I mean, pretend the other person is a bitch—in order to hide the truth from themselves that they are, in fact, a bitch.'

'And guess what, Jessica?' [*She gestures to herself*] '… You're a bitch.'

She stops crying, and I let her share my fries.

▼ ▼ ▼ ▼ ▼

FOOD
DIDEM CAIA

Scene: A room. The humidity of a summer's night drifts through the window and illuminates the space, which isn't literal, but an amalgamation of household essentials.

There is a large bed positioned in the centre. Crisp white sheets, not a crease. On this bed are scattered bluebell petals.

On one side of the bed is a stainless-steel oven/stove and on the other side is a dining table covered with health magazines and luxurious products such as lavender soap. A bottle of bleach is also visible.

The walls of the space are covered in various paintings, quite conservative and mainly of landscapes, none particularly attractive.

On the stove a small pot is on a high boil and the sound is abrasive. The flames hiss every time the water bubbles too rebelliously.

The oven is on, but the dish inside is obscured from our view.

ANNIE, a young woman, sits at the foot of the bed with her legs tucked elegantly beneath her. She wears a white bathrobe and folds her newly washed underwear, of which every pair is white.

Apparently vacuuming at five a.m. isn't very reasonable, at least this is what I gathered from the profane language the neighbour served me this morning. Sleeplessness strikes me sporadically, but on this day I'm pleased that I've finished my tasks and am ready to focus my attention on you and you alone.

On the way home I bought the lavender soap. Not only does it give my skin the glow of a glazed cheesecake, but studies have shown that it has the ability to soothe a racing mind. You know how I get in times of complete excitement, don't you? And this was truly a day of excitement, a day worthy of lavender soap.

Food

ANNIE rises and places her tower of meticulously folded underwear on the dining table.

I decided to wear my blazer to the interview, the one with the shoulder pads. And I paired it with that skirt that flatters my bottom half. The bottom half you're so fond of putting your mark on.

Beat.

There were other women there, of course. Five in total, scattered, spaces between us, worlds between us. Their restless feet were waiting to get in and get out. Restless feet in red shoes. Red says confidence, red says, 'I'm here'. Then there were those who'd chosen to wear runners, probably to mask their bad pedicures and neglected skin. Clogs, loafers, thongs… Thongs, to a job interview?

Beat.

Perhaps that particular female didn't get the memo, allure is manufactured. In crucial moments such as those, one needs to sell themselves, to prove themselves, because actually every event that life offers is a chance to *show*. Strength, diplomacy, people skills. And I didn't squander my opportunity.

Being part of a magazine that promotes healthy eating and a healthy image is a rarity. Perhaps I'll need to vary my cooking skills, learn how to branch out and create new dishes, so that I'll be able transfer those physical sensations of eating and tasting into captivating descriptions. To entice people, entice them into enjoying their food.

And when I begin this job, I will do it with the absolute best part of myself, the most sensual, spiritual, hungry part of myself.

You're well-acquainted with that side, aren't you? My ravenous side. My abandon, my submission, my surrender in the comfort of your approval.

How I'm craving you now. Looking forward to 'you know'. Tonight is our night, every other night of the week is redundant, and it's only when you come and steal my loneliness and tame me with your warmth, that I feel worthy of showing myself and lavender-soaping myself in preparation for the contact.

    Beat.

I think I've really got the skill to do this job. The insight. The allure.
Allure is important, allure is something a female becomes acquainted with the first time her mother brushes her hair, the first time she wears lipstick, the first time she tastes the sweet satisfaction of warm honey milk.

    Beat.

If my mum was still here, she would bask in the glory of her daughter's first proper job. I would say, 'Mum, I walked right into that meeting room and planted my feet within the metaphorical earth, just to really feel I was present in the room, not allowing my anxiety to thrust me into the future of, well, getting the job'.

    ANNIE motions toward the oven and opens it. She smells the dish.

You're on your way, aren't you?
You're rising in anticipation of tonight, I can feel it. I know you, I know you so well. I don't mind where we begin. We can begin at the table and move to the bed, or begin at the bed and finish on the table.

    Beat.

I just want to tell you about my day. Press you to my lips in between telling you about my day. I enjoy watching you be silent as you listen to me, not rejecting my stories. You'd listen to me all night if that were what I wanted. You're so available.

    Obscured from the audience, ANNIE slips off her robe. She is wearing a long red negligee.

    She re-appears and, using a tea towel, retrieves a large cake

Food

tin from the oven and puts it on the dining table.

She takes the cake out of the tin and places it onto a plate. It is a righteous work of art.

Taking the small pot off the stove, ANNIE drizzles dark ooze onto the cake. It dribbles effortlessly over the decadent dessert, her body moving in circular motions as she performs this action.

I'm glad I can see and touch and smell and taste you, have purpose with you.

She draws back her bedsheets, the petals falling to the ground.

I think I'd like to begin in the bed.

She carries the large cake to bed with her.

Have you sit here in bed with me, comfort me, calm me, fill me with hope and ambition, with anticipation for tomorrow and tomorrow and tomorrow. Fill me, fill me up, do it well so it lasts. Make it last, at least until next time.

ANNIE devours the cake. Though she has a fork, she seems to be enjoying the physical action of grabbing, tearing and sucking. She immerses herself in the act of absolute chocolate carnage, switching between fast and slow motions, gorging and nibbling, allowing her whole being to be affected, not just her mouth.

Her insatiability doesn't lessen as the lights slowly fade and we bear witness to the tumultuous culmination, a mixture of utter ecstasy and fear.

▼ ▼ ▼ ▼ ▼

B-T-DUBS MUM...
LUCY COLEMAN

Note: With the exception of the chaplain, all italics are Mel doing the voice of her mother.

Mel. 17.

It's 6:42, the ad break comes on for Neighbours, Mum turns the volume down and asks, *do you still have to go to mass?*

Yeah.

She just stares at me trying to work out from my apathetic expression as to whether I'm telling the truth or not. Which is confusing cuz I don't understand why she gives a shit.

Yeah I do Mum. I find it really interesting.

She says nothing and looks back at the telly.

Oh... and um b-t-dubs bitch it's mandatory so I have to go.

[Mock chaplain voice] *Let him in. Fill your heart with the light and the joy that Jesus wants to betroth on you. Only then will you reap the true wonders of what the world can really offer.*

You know what I would love to be betrothed with? Usher's tenderly caressing my boobies. Can you do that for me God? Cheers, thanks mate.

[Mum] *What's Kelly up to?*

I shrug.

Why don't you ask her on facebook Mum? You added her last week along with ten of my other friends, which was not the slightest bit embarrassing.

I haven't seen her around much. Have you had a falling out?

B-T-Dubs Mum...

No.

Toadie's face reappears on the screen and she turns the volume back up.

Oh um, actually we did Mum. You know the other night when I said me and Kel were having a sleepover and watching *She's the Man* and I got crook from the dodgy Chinese food we ate. Well I actually went to this party, off my tits on Midori and double black Smirnoff, and told Kel that I thought her boyfriend was a dumb cunt pinger head who looked like an uglier version of Ed Sheeran. Which I didn't even think was humanly possible. Then Kel told me that I was a virgin loser who wouldn't even be able to get a boyfriend if I went down to the Salvos and told all the junkees that my scung gunk tasted like ice.

Pause.

What's for dinner?

Pause.

Mum?

Leftovers. You can do it yourself.

[*Hopeful*] Takeaways?

She doesn't even respond. Just stares at Toadie's fat fuck head bobbing around on TV.

Hey Mum I've been thinking about uni next year—

Shh not now.

...I don't think I want to study veterinarian science anymore.

Yes you do. Well talk about it later.

Pause.

THE VOICES PROJECT: ENCORE EDITION

I'm going to move to New York City and become a famous vagina artist. I've got it all planned out. For my first artwork I'm going to take all these photos of my vulva and then collage them to make a big picture of Tony Abbot's face. Below will read the caption, 'Fist yourself then die fucktard!'

What do you think Mum?

Oh Melanie, I think that's a great idea! I'll pay for your rent and flights for the first year. I hear Brooklyn's the place to be. If it's your art that you're truly wuely passionate about then you have to follow your heart darl!

Oh my god! Thanks so much Mum! You're the best.

I told Mr Cliff about my plans to move to New York City. He's like the only teacher that doesn't hang out in the staff room all day and communally masturbate to pictures of Jaden Smith. And he's actually the most delightfully-smelling man alive. He just, he just, smells like... Man. Like a Man. Just like this real... Man. When he leans over my shoulder to help me with my Maths I subtly inhale through my nostrils to get a big wiff and then I get this tremendous urge to reach my hand across and gently stroke his arm hairs...

Anyway. Basically Mr Cliff thinks it's a great idea and he's all for it.

Ad comes on again.

What were you saying about uni?

Um. That maybe I... like not... ahh—

You're a smart girl Melanie. Don't throw that away and do something stupid for God's sake.

Yeah nah I know Mum... Did I tell you Aliesha had another baby?

Netball Aliesha?

Yeah.

B-T-Dubs Mum...

That's disgusting! You're not having sex are you?

Yeah I am. But no worries Mum I'd just get an abortion.

She stares at me blank. I can't tell if she's getting real angry or if she's just really confused.

Back on. Volume up.

I just told you that I'm having sex and if I got pregnant I'd have an abortion. It's good to know you're pro-choice, but do you not have anything to say? Like use a condom, or don't have sex, you will get Chlamydia and die. Or, he'd better be a nice young man who treats you with the upmost respect that you deserve Melanie. Uh. What am I saying? Sorry Mum, I should realize that Susan and Carl's marital problems are your first priority.

Pause.

I told the pastor I left my last tampon in for 15 days to see if I could suicide from TSS. I didn't actually want to suicide it was more just a mythbusting experiment really. He told me that he understood my urges to be closer to God, but I must resist and continue God's work on earth in good grace. Good grace! HA!

I seeked sweet revenge and contaminated the holy water with my period blood. And I didn't just dunk my tampon in the chalice like a teabag. I squatted over it, and squeezed my uterus as hard as I could to push out some nice fresh clots. The kind that when you pull out your tampon and it has a good fling it slings the clump of blood all over the back of the toilet door.

Pause.

Me and Kel did have a fight.

No Response.

Pause.

It actually kind of backfired though cuz Mr Cliff caught me and told me I should go see a psychiatrist. The man that I'm most in love with in the entire world caught me with my pants down fuckin' pushing fresh clots out into the school chalice! I was so mortified that I haven't been back to Maths in six weeks. He emailed me a bunch of times to tell me that it's fine, he hasn't told anyone and I should just come back to class.

    Pause.

Mum?

Mum.

    Pause.

Hey Mum?

How good was that episode last week Mum where Carl got his dick out in the café and pissed on all the customers.

Melanie!

What?

Sorry Mum. Susan and Carl are having a really rough time, I guess I should try and be more compassionate and stop interrupting. Oh thank fuck, END CREDITS.

Mum? Mum? Hey Mum? Mum? Mum? Mum?

WHAAAAAATTTTT??????

    Long pause. Mel stares back at her Mum. Her mouth opens to say something… then she stops herself.

She turns the TV off.

    Pause.

… Nothing.

B-T-Dubs Mum...

Pause.

Mr Cliff was forced to tell the Dean why I'd stopped going to class and I got suspended last week. And I may or may not have told him to go fuck himself... Cuz I'm an idiot... And I haven't had sex. I *am* a virgin loser. And I have no friends... Cuz Kel hates me. And she's more popular than I am so now everyone hates me.

Pause.

We hear the ping of the microwave. Mel calls out to her Mum in the Kitchen:

Hey Mum? If you're re-heating some spag bol, can you do some for me too please?

Next stop New York motherfuckers.

▼ ▼ ▼ ▼ ▼

WILLIAM BURROUGHS' WIFE
GRACE DE MORGAN

A half-naked seventeen-year-old boy, ANDY, stands onstage, an apple on top of his head.
He tries to balance it for as long as he can.
A shirt lies on the floor at his feet. A blanket is folded off to the side.

Would you let me talk? Would you let me talk? Would you let me— ?

That story. That story you told me. It *is* relevant. If you let me explain you'd see why.

You're attractive. You're hot. Everyone thinks so. That *Twilight* chick looks like a ferret in comparison to you. What do you want me to say?

I don't know. I don't know what's wrong. I'm not scared. Something's off. It's not that I don't want to. I do, it's just…

You look so much like her. The dark hair, the eyes. And this room, this room is too much like a Mexican hovel. It's strange because I usually love it here. The dusty shelves, the yellowing couch, the weird corkboard floor. But now, it's so… it's too…

I think about her a lot. I think about why she did it. There's a part of me that wants to travel back in time, shake her and yell, 'Stop! What are you doing? Are you mental?' Because no guy is worth that, right? No guy— no matter how funny or lovely or arty or hot. Or maybe there are exceptions. Maybe, I'm… I don't know.

Are you going? Why are you going? Don't go. Dana, we're not done here. I want to explain. Just give me a minute to think. Just let me figure something out. You're supposed to help me figure this out. You're supposed to listen. Who else am I going to talk to about this? Mum? Call up Dad on his way to sell shitty homewares in South America?

I get it if you want to go. Just tell me when I can see you next. Tell me when this is going to be okay. Because it has to be okay. It needs to be okay. If you don't look at me in the corridors, who else will?

The lights change and he wraps himself in the blanket.

It's already five or six weeks into first term. It's late enough that we're already choosing extra texts, but early enough that the guys in my year haven't quite got over the fact that we have girls around. Barker has a fresh intake of boobs and there are erections aplenty.

Anyway here we are in third period English with Mr Lewis, and while I watch Kurt Daniels playing with his fly, you lean in and ask me what extra texts I've chosen. I haven't even thought about it, but the grin on your face tells me you have. So I shrug and ask what you're doing.

You open your ugly, lime-green folder and nudge a copy of *Naked Lunch* by Burroughs towards me.
'You know he killed his wife? Tried to shoot an apple off her head. Missed. Some people said it was an accident. Others said he did it on purpose because he was gay and didn't want her around anymore.'
I laugh because I don't know what to say. And while you invite me over to your house to watch the movie version of it, I just think about what woman would put an apple on her head and let her husband point a gun at her and shoot.

In your TV room you stand on a chair and try to find your dad's collection of Cronenberg DVDs on the bookshelf. I wonder if I should tell the guys I came here. Halfway through first term and I'm already inside the hot new chick's house. I know how they'd react:
'Did she put out?'
'You cop a feel?'
'She give you a handy, Andy?'

THE VOICES PROJECT: ENCORE EDITION

Maybe I won't tell them. I don't want them to hassle us, have you pull away. But then again…

You grumble under your breath as your search leads you nowhere. I tell you that it's okay, how about we download it instead? You shake your head and tell me that's stealing. I laugh, not because I'm really laughing at you, but because you're strong and you surprise me and I love that.

You look a little to your right and spot *Naked Lunch* on a dusty shelf above you. You lift your hands above your head and I watch as your tartan skirt rises from your thighs to just a little below your bum. I can see the bottom of your small black undies.

I wait for something to click, some feeling. I wait for it, I wait, I…

> *The lights change. ANDY puts the blanket and apple down and the shirt on.*

Back at school, you sit on the grass while I lie down, my head in your lap. You've been my girlfriend for over three months now. I go over to yours every Friday night and we watch movies in your overly warm TV room. It's my favourite part of the week because there in that small room with you— with the television blaring— there's peace, there's order. I'm home.

People at school have been calling us 'Dandy'— Dana and Andy. I think it's lame, but you don't seem to care. You're so chilled and always seem to talk me down. Like that time Miss Wood confiscated my iPhone then lost it, or the time Dad and Tina turned up at my soccer game as if that was cool and we were one big happy family.

But here on the warm grass, cushioned by your heat, I wonder how I could have been upset about anything… ever.

It's my birthday tomorrow and you tell me to come over tonight so I can get my present. You make me guess what it is. A new iPhone? You make a loud buzzer noise and tell me to guess again. I let my eyes wander around the playground as I try to think what you could afford. But instead of finding an answer I find Martin Hobbs eating an apple and leering at Double Double Debbie. Even though we're on the other side of the grass, I can hear him crunching, breaking the apple's skin with his perfect white teeth. I don't think anything, a feeling seems to short-circuit past my brain straight to…

'Wrong!' you giggle, 'Guess again'.
I didn't think I'd said anything.

   The lights change and ANDY picks up the apple.

You're in the doorway wearing a lacy nightie. You offer me an apple like I'm a teacher and you're a naughty schoolgirl. But you're not a naughty schoolgirl, you're a schoolgirl, a schoolgirl who's telling me she's ready and has been for a while.

You look really pretty. Your hair, your lips, your skin. You smell like vanilla. You ask if I like my present. And I want to say yes. I want to see you in that nightie and think, 'Fuck, that's my girlfriend. My girlfriend dressed up in suspenders and came to my door offering an apple like we're in fucking *Cruel Intentions.*'

I want to look at you the way you're looking at me now. I want to… I guess… Maybe if I…

   ANDY drops the apple and takes his shirt off.

Our clothes start falling to the floor and you fall back onto the threadbare couch and I know this is my cue, this is the time, but I see the apple you brought dropped on the ground and I can't stop thinking about William Burroughs' wife and why she'd put that apple on her head. The room starts shrinking and it's hard to breathe—was it complete trust, was she sacrificing herself, was she desperate? But instead of just ripping off your undies and going for it, I pull the blanket off the back of the couch and wrap it around you. I transform you from flirt to fat caterpillar in under five seconds.

And I see the confusion in your eyes and I see the rising wave

of rejection threatening to drown you and I see the apple placed on top of your head.
But I won't shoot, Dana. Will you?

▼ ▼ ▼ ▼ ▼

RUPTURE

KENDALL FEAVER

SHANNON, *seventeen years old.*

It started with a tiny crack.

A hole.

And I didn't sew it up straight away. I let it settle there. Let new ideas squeeze in.

I'll consider them, I thought. I'll consider them. And then I'll cover it back up. Pretend it never happened.

But the crack grew, and grew, and then there were more of them, giant gaping gashes too big to mend, and now… there's a canyon in our living room. It stretches from the couch right to the kitchen, and Mum stands on the other side, tapping at her watch, Sunday best, hat upon her head:

Shannon. Let's go.

But I can't move. My feet won't walk me out the door.

She stares at me. She knows something's wrong. I can see her brain working overtime, trawling through that massive list of teenage indiscretions. Did I fail a test? Am I pregnant? A junkie? Or worse… a *lesbian*?

'Mum… I—'

It's stuck. Sitting in my gut. I need to— I have to— I do.

'Mum. I don't want to go to church anymore.'

She sits down. Hard. Like I've hit her in the stomach. Drawn a gun and shot it.

Why? She's saying, *Why?*

And I don't know how to explain it to her—how to break it to her—that the beliefs she's held all her life make as little sense to me as ancient Greek or American football.

Belief for Mum is passion. She likes passion. Could understand passion. If I joined a cult, drenched myself in chicken blood, wrapped my legs around an ailing prophet and became his sixteenth wife… eventually, she'd let it pass. But to not believe in anything. To not believe at all. *That* she can't understand.

For a week, she thinks it's a phase. Like leg warmers, or Zumba.

You'll get over it, she says. *You'll get over it.*

But the crack has gotten bigger. It's split the backyard in two, swallowed up the pot plants and the pets, Monty's barking from the deep abyss, and Mum stands on the other side, tapping at her watch, Sunday best, hat upon her head:

Shannon. Let's go.

But I stay.

I stay and she… she cries. Like I've hurt her. Like I'm doing this to her.

'Mum?'
Don't.
'Please?'
Don't.

She's gone. Out the door, down the street, past the school to the place I've gone every Sunday since I was born.

Shit.

Bad daughter. Selfish daughter. And I'm putting on my shoes and socks, I'm grabbing my coat, I'm going after her, when she walks back in with Pastor Fred.

Rupture

Pastor Fred. Old, balding man who belts his pants close to his armpits. When I was little, I thought he was Santa Claus. I could never find the reindeer but I knew he had a giant book that told him who was naughty and who was nice, and every Sunday (not just at Christmas) you'd kneel in front of him, clasp your hands together, and tell him everything you wanted: world peace… no poverty… more Christians in Africa… a pony.

And now he's in my living room, chair legs straddle the precipice, and Mum is serving tea. She cuts him a piece of cake and he rests it on his belly. Then he leans in towards me, eyes on mine, firm, serious:

Can I talk to Shannon?

I'm confused, because I'm sitting right in front of him, but he leans in closer— God, his breath could melt the icecaps— and he places one hand on my head, raises the other one above it and bellows:

Release Shannon! Deliver her to us! Free her from your grip!

At first, nothing happens. Then I shake a little, drool out the side of my mouth, feel my eyes roll into the back of my head, and then—

I laugh! I laugh, I laugh— I can't stop— but no-one else is smiling.

He tries again, and again, but my head doesn't spin around, I'm not swearing or speaking foreign languages and I don't vomit on the floor. So Pastor Fred gives up. He wipes the sweat from his face, and leaves with his Bible and his belly and half a glad-wrapped cake.

Mum screams at me:

Have you no shame?
Do you think this is a joke?
Do you know where people like you end up?!

Sydney, apparently. I'm catching the overnight train. There's no eternal fire or red-skinned Satan, but my father's there, the backslidden one, and Mum thinks that's bad enough. With liberal supervision she imagines I'll drink wine and smoke pot, read Nietzsche and sleep with bearded men who'll pass me around like coleslaw at a picnic.

I put my things into a suitcase and she acts like she doesn't care. She vacuums, puts the rugs outside to beat them, throws scraps down to Monty and dusts all of the windows. But right before I leave, she sneaks into my room and carefully repacks. She matches all my dresses to my shoes and to my bags, putting them on hangers so I don't mess up her handiwork.

On top, she rests the old family Bible—I object—but she says it's a family heirloom, and who else does she have to pass it on to? I want to grab her, want to hug her goodbye, but she's dusting again, and she still has seven windows.

At the train station, I flick to the back where the names of five generations are inscribed in perfect cursive. Whole lives bound up in this book, and me, trying to live my life without it. And I realise that the gaping hole's still there. Because when you stop believing, it's like a friend has died. And not just any friend, this superhero dude called Jesus who has amazing hair and lives inside your heart. And I feel so alone, so I start to pray, and I think— Shit, I can't do that anymore. And then I think of all the other things that I can't do. Who will I speak to when I'm all alone? Where will I get married? Whose name am I supposed to shout out during sex?!

I'm dizzy, and the ground is moving like it's about to swallow me up. I can't breathe. I'm scared. And for a moment, I want to go back. Now I've torn everything up, there's nothing… there's nothing… there's nothing left to tie it all together. I wait for trees to bend and break, for mountains to crumble, for the sky to cave in without someone keeping it upright, but—

It doesn't.

It doesn't change.

Rupture

The trees are firm.

Mountains tall.

And they stay where they've always been.

Stars. Thousands of them.

Gleaming. Glittering. Beautiful. Bright.

▼ ▼ ▼ ▼ ▼

BOYS DON'T BELIEVE IN FAIRIES
JOSH FORWARD

JULES, a seventeen-year-old boy, shuffles on stage slowly with a torch and stands by the trunk of a red gum tree. He's wearing a sloppy jumper covered in stains. He looks around nervously, frightened of something. He looks up at the tree.

Bloody freezing…

The wind blows. A branch creaks.

Hello? Who's there? Are you there?

I know it's early. I woke up because I heard a bunyip whispering in my ear. I don't speak bunyip so I have no idea what it was saying. But I heard it say your name. I think you might be in trouble or something. Wherever it is in the world you fucked off to. You hurt or something? Alone? Homesick? You coming back? Huh? I don't know what you expect me to do about it. We don't even know where the fuck you are.

JULES walks the stage. Stopping every now and again to dig.

You know, it's your fault the fog reminds me of bunyips. I slipped on the mossy rocks on the bottom of the creek and fell into the water. I wasn't even knee-deep but I was convinced I was going to drown, screaming and thrashing about. You just yelled, 'Watch out for the bunyip! It'll rip out your eyeballs and make you watch yourself drown before it drags you away into the eternal fog!' Was it you who finally pulled me from the water? Or Dad? Or maybe the bunyip did drag me away.

I believed you. I was always so bloody gullible, but only to you. It wasn't until Year Eight that I realised honey wasn't just bee poo. Makes me wonder about all that stuff you said to me before you left. Or were they just like the bunyip stories? But when I tried to tell you about the fairies I saw in the trees you

Boys Don't Believe in Fairies

just laughed at me and said, 'Come on, Jules. Grow some balls because the tits aren't coming. Boys don't believe in fairies.'

I never mentioned them again.

I did see those fairies though. Dancing on the red gums. It was dark and early like it is now. I was barely awake and heard the bunyip howling from the creek. Like I dreamt this morning. I'm not stupid enough to think they ever actually existed, but sometimes when it's cold and it's just about to rain, the fog slides like a sheet through the mountains and along the creek and it's like there's a bunyip steering it along.

He stops digging.

Bitsy threw up on my bed so I slept in yours tonight. I hope that's okay. Not like you're using it. Bitsy hates me. I have no idea how such a tiny cat can produce so much vomit. Your room doesn't even smell like you anymore. Just the smell of crisp clean linen that Mum keeps changing for no reason.

She'll have a fit if she knows I slept in your room. A few weeks ago I sat at the spot you usually sit at the table and Mum just went wide-eyed and said in her singsong voice, 'Oh. That's not where you usually sit', but I know she meant 'Why are you sitting in Aaron's seat?' I ended up moving back to my seat after I got a glass of water.

He starts digging again.

You were in my dream.

It was a memory. I was chasing you through the trees near the house and it was so hot that we pretended that if we stayed in the sun for more than a second, we would burst into flames. So we jumped under the trees, from shadow to shadow.

I was carrying an old lunch box and we both had scrunched-up pieces of paper clenched in our fists that contained a secret we were keeping from one another. We found a shady spot, placed our secrets in the box and buried them under a tree. We agreed that we'd unearth it in fifty years and read each other's secret. Do you remember your secret? Do you even care what mine is?

That's where the dream turned from a memory into something stranger. After burying our secrets we ran off again into the maze of eucalypt trees with the earth under our fingernails as the only evidence of our buried secrets. We came to that dirt patch where nothing would ever grow no matter how many times Dad tried, remember that? You and Dad called it the cricket pitch. In my dream you ran out into the centre of it and I was too scared to follow. I called out, warning you against the hot sun. I think by this stage we weren't young anymore, as though all the running had aged us into who we are now, so it was your tall figure that was running through the cricket pitch. You didn't burn, you just kind of started to dry up. I watch your thin lips go white, the hair on your arms and legs snapped off like twigs, and your dark brown eyes dried up like snails covered in salt. You put your foot down to run, and your leg cracked and shattered at the impact. You fell and smashed into the ground, crumbling like fallen pottery. Come back! Come back! I shouted and I shouted until I was drowned out by the howl of the bunyip in my ear. But it wasn't a bunyip. It was Bisty.

Freaking Bitsy.

He stops digging.

He got all excited because he heard me in your room. He thought you were home again. Even fucking Bitsy misses you!

I could see the tree from your window. The red gum we buried our secrets under. Same tree where you fell out when that sleeping possum scared the crap out of you and your arm broke.

The tree's marked with a little X now. Buzz Killington next door said, 'There's a substantial root system interfering with the pipes'. So it's coming down.

That's why I'm here. I remembered the secret. I have to know what it is before the tree gets taken away.

Boys Don't Believe in Fairies

I'm wearing your jumper. I hope that's okay. The one I got choc-top stains all over it when I wore it to the movies that time to impress Veronica Tilly, and you got so mad you farted on my toothbrush. Didn't matter anyway. She told me that she didn't want to go out with me because I was too boring.

He looks around, returns to a hole he's already dug and looks again with the torch.

Maybe I'll never know your secret. Even if you come back, you might not even remember. If you come back I promise I'll tell you mine. I haven't told anyone. Just you and the tree.

He rests against the tree.

You must have thousands of secrets now. You kept taking off to the other side of the planet a secret, until you were gone. I wish I could see you, open up your head and just rifle through your head like a rolodex. I wish I was there filling it with you. We could share the same secrets.

It starts to rain. He doesn't budge.

A little bit of rain never hurt anybody—even if it makes the red gums look like they're bleeding.

The fog is close now. It's thick. Like an army of bunyips. Imagine for a second it was true. That there were bunyips hiding in the fog ready to devour me. The fog would grow thicker, creep closer, envelop the mulberry tree first, then the compost bin, and then by the time it reached the clothes line their hands would be close enough to grab me. Pull me into the river and into waters I never knew were so deep. Where it's so dark I can't even see my hands. Can't even tell if the hands are mine or the bunyips' pulling me down. Who would pull me out? It would have to be the fairies.

They'd rally themselves, fleeing from the bleeding trees, put their warm tiny hands on my body until I was covered in them. They'd lift me from the wet, into the sky, so high the roof of our house is lost under a canopy of trees, above the clouds and into the sun. They'd be tucked under my neck and on my shoulder, crane their necks to whisper into my ear. They know your secrets. They know where you are. They know my secrets too. To them our secrets are boring and make them giggle. We'd meet up and laugh, you'd tell me your stories, you'd see the fairies and laugh that I'd been right all along. There'd be no bunyips, just fairies.

    JULES stands up.

It's cold and I'm wet. I think I'll go back to bed.

I know. Don't be silly, boys don't believe in fairies.

▼ ▼ ▼ ▼ ▼

MEAT
SUNDAY EMERSON GULLIFER

A seventeen-year-old boy.
A co-educational boarding school a few hours outside of an Australian city.
Summer.

Meat
flayed and cooking.
World slowly spinning.
What I wouldn't do for a fucking kebab.

Two a.m.
and we're waiting for them
cameras ready
their tits are exposed.
Bouncing
fresh meat
running
shrieking
shielding themselves
flashes lighting up their retreating arses.

It's not a dare.
It's tradition.

Dark outside
no sign of security
and we're running fast
hard
naked across the oval.
Torches flicker
and I hear the boys around me.

Up ahead
a boarding house
the girls
clothed
inside now
hanging out windows.
Panting.
Waiting.

*Oi Matthews you prick
catch up!*

Biology bores.
Been wearing the same pants all term
haven't washed them once
good thing about school uniforms, hey Miss?
Grey
no-one can tell.

Rugby scrums slam.
Saturday sport.
*Ka mate ka mate
ka ora ka ora.*

Bet she likes it hard and fast
up against the wall
behind the chapel
in the cloisters
in the vestibule.

Towers and trophies
ovals and statues
steaks in trays and powdered eggs.
And us.
Girls on one end
boys on the other
teachers thrown in.

Meat

Borrow Dad's car
home for a bit
take it for a ride.
Away in London
he'll never know.
House to myself for the weekend
I could get used to this.

Road running slick
and tram tracks divided.
A screech and
a hiss and
a slam and
a crack.
I'm not looking when it hits.

And this man
I think he's homeless
is just standing there.
Crying.
Not weeping
not just like a few tears and shit.
He's wailing.
Standing on the street
wailing like a baby.

His whole body is shaking.

And I say
Mate.
Mate I'm sorry about your dog.
Mate I'm sorry.

And he's holding its crumpled black body in his arms.
And its legs are broken
and it's oozing blood
and it's yelping

and it doesn't have long.

Mate I'm
I'm so sorry.

Back broken.
Guts spewing and bowels heaving
brains splattered across the ground
Eyes oozing jelly.

Bitumen baking
and torn apart.
Ripped.
Bones
cracked
and
beaten
splintered
shrapnel.

Smashed souvlaki and blood pooling in the gutter.

Mate.
Mate I'm sorry about your dog.
Mate I'm sorry.

Yeah just a quiet weekend at home with the family
Sir.

What do you think you'll eat tonight? Let's talk about that.
Fuck off Byron you shit.
I just find it interesting what people eat.
It's all the same though isn't it.
And the steaks in vats of gravy
bubbling
oozing
sweltering
yelping

Meat

And it doesn't have long.

And the homeless man
keeps crying.
And I keep
eating
sleeping
pissing
scratching
sweating
wanking
learning.

Thursday night
cutlets for dinner.
Grey chunks of meat
swimming in goo
chewy
stringy
gristly
oozing
vomitous.
Guts spewing and bowels heaving
brains splattered across the ground
Eyes oozing jelly.
Retching in the bushes outside the dining hall.
—Fuck off Byron you shit.

There's a whisper
that night
a whisper making the rounds
just a peep
just a morsel
a nugget that grows.
Tonight's the night.
Boys growing rowdy

Boys growing itchy
skin crawling
sweat dripping
we smell blood.

Housemaster's out for the evening.
Got a date with the missus sir?
Gonna get some action sir?
Taking her somewhere nice sir?
Gonna dress like that sir?
Make some effort sir.
—*Yeah alright alright.*

And then it's go time.

Ka mate ka mate
ka ora ka ora.

Across the grass
in their boarding house
girls
clothed
inside now
hanging out windows.
Panting.
Waiting.

And the chant
it builds.
Ka mate ka mate
ka ora ka ora.

Blood pumping
Neurons firing
Thoughts racing
Girls provoking

Ka mate ka mate

Meat

ka ora ka ora
ka mate ka mate
ka ora ka ora.

It's Byron
pale ridiculous Byron
desperate to impress.
—Fuck off Byron you shit.
Picks up a chair
window turns shrapnel.

It feels like there's a moment
—Mate I'm sorry
a brief second
—I'm sorry about your dog
before hell breaks loose.

Hands close and fists connect
as shoes and pool cues
lamps and books
bats and balls
turn militant.
The heat is overwhelming and
the boys
we turn on each other
snarling
jostling
joking
fighting
beating
hurling
rioting
consuming.

I trip.
I go down
and a boot

connects
with my head.

And this man
I think he's homeless
is just standing there.
Crying.
Not weeping
not just like a few tears and shit.
He's wailing.
Standing on the street
wailing like a baby.

His whole body is shaking.

I'm not looking when it hits.

Sirens.
Flashing.
Dad's in London
but I'm here.
And there's a dog standing over me
small
black
and energetic.
Licks my face
licks my tongue
quivers against my chest.
I thought it was

Smashed souvlaki and blood pooling in the gutter.

Meat
flayed and cooking.
World slowly spinning.
What I wouldn't do for a fucking kebab.

▼ ▼ ▼ ▼ ▼

A note from the playwright

The words *'Ka mate ka mate, ka ora ka ora'* are from a widely known haka, the traditional chant performed by the New Zealand All Blacks rugby team, which is internationally associated with New Zealand and rugby culture. It was, however, composed by Te Rauparaha, chief of the Māori North Island tribal group, Ngāti Toa, in the 1800s.

▼ ▼ ▼ ▼ ▼

ANYU*

*Hungarian word for 'mother'

ZSUZSANNA IHAR

A girl, IRÉN, sits next to a table with a lace tablecloth in an apartment kitchen; she is scrubbing a dirty plate with detergent and soap. As the monologue progresses the scrubbing gets increasingly frantic, and in tempo with her words.

The milk has gone sour again.
On the neat white tablecloth with her fingerprints,
her grease,
her spit,
her bile,
her sweat still there,
forming yellow sighs *spilling* into the lace.

Minden piszkos.
Minden szennyezett.

It was supposed to be easy.
Come into her apartment,
start with the bleach,
the detergent,
the trash bags,
so we could have the flat on the market by Monday.
At the latest.

It was supposed to be that easy, Elliott.
All I wanted was the cleanness.
I was owed spotless countertops,
stainless steel pots
and showroom-quality porcelain.

Anyu

Instead, there are hairline cracks on the plates,
cartons of curdled milk,
feral minced-meat pies.
Fuck.
It's a mess and she's gone.
Egy mocskos, koszos nő volt.

    Beat.

But you know what that bitch did?
In the kitchen right,
there was still a careful arrangement of last night's dinner.
It was left there.
The meal she never chewed or swallowed down
before her pulse ate itself.

It *still* fucks me up.
Seeing the leftovers of skin cells,
dandruff,
cutlery with oil stains,
dentures,
strands of hair in mashed potatoes.
The leftovers.

I mean,
how many families come home
after the emergency room,
the funeral home,
the retirement village,
and see the unfinished meal and it triggers them to think,
about, about decomposition,
marriages,
affairs,
rotting,
perishables,
breakdowns,
regrets,

secrets,
midlife crises,
mortgages,
spoilage.
Probably not the vast majority.
But I did.

For me,
it's not the mementos,
the photos taken on the west coast,
the heirlooms,
the 'forever'-engraved bracelets,
which always end up at Vinnies anyway,
that remind us.

It's the stains on mattresses,
the grime on white plates,
the used teeth floss,
the cum stains on bedsheets,
the piss stains from childhood nightmares
still on the blankets.

It's those leftovers,
those residues,
the unfinished meals that make it so hard to forget.
She wanted to remind us Elliott,
and I just want to fucking forget.

She was a cunning cunt, wasn't she?

    Beat.

The milk was always sour.
There is still a carton left in the fridge.
She never threw it out.
Milk is meant to be sweet,
our taste of lightness,

Anyu

whiteness,
it is meant to be the protein arms
wrapping around our bellies.

   Beat.

Mum's milk was never sweet.
Remember how the spit curdled on the corners of her mouth
and how we had to clean it off?
White curd on her blood-red senile gums,
like some fungal growth on lamb chops.
It was fucking rank.

   Beat.

Egy hülye picsa volt, egy hülye kurva volt.

I've been scrubbing the dishes,
my fingers are raw and scabbing,
you should be helping out.
You should be here.
Remember how we used to clean her,
scrub her,
feed her,
burp her like a fucking brain-dead infant?
Who was the mother
and who was the liability?
I always had to be the pleasant daughter,
the generous daughter,
the tired and hopeless daughter.
You saw those small beads of black in her eyes,
like blowflies,
that's how fucking close she was to death even back then.

There is a bowl of congealed and dried-up broth on the
counter, and I can't even touch it Elliott.
It's as if I was looking at her skin,
how I didn't know whether

whether she was swarmed by dark age spots
or carrion insects, attracted to the odour, the stench
that settles when a human decides to become an animal again.

She was vile.

    Beat.

She was my mum.

    Beat.

Az anyukám volt.

    Beat.

It's everywhere,
the steak-sauce-kissed napkins,
hairline crack marks on mugs,
the spoilage of fruit like a toxic spill of sugars,
acids
and sweetness.
The dirt, the stains, the grime.
Sometimes I see them as traces of 'I am sorry';
'I am sorry Susan'; 'I am sorry sweetheart';
sometimes I see them as things I'll never clean off.

    Beat.

You were there.
You were there
when it got so fucked up
that she couldn't recall my name.
It was left rotting on the tip of her tongue.
And I just shook her;
I couldn't stop shaking her,
I couldn't stop shaking her
as if I could disintegrate her whole body.
Because she became landfill.

Anyu

She became trash.
And she was meant to be my mum.

Utáltam ot, gyűlöltem őt.

Remember how she couldn't control herself,
the coughing,
the gases,
the tears;
how she cried,
how she wailed like some fucked-up
mid-slaughter animal.
And it was over me.
I know it was over me.

I was the fat,
the filth,
a tiny death within her,
and it was bore water that broke when I was born;
dirty and undrinkable,
so she refused to keep me from spoiling,
keep me from going off
like everything else in her,
around her.
I just needed to be held.
She never held me.

    Beat.

I need to clean
I need this to be clean
I need this.

    Beat.

Why was the milk always so sour, Elliott?

    Beat.

I had this theory when we were kids
that there is universal attraction of
clumping, of coming together, of compression
to fill spaces, to fill emptiness
like food scraps in landfill,
or bodies thrown upon bodies,
dirt thrown on the grave
mass on mass.
It's what makes gravity so fucking powerful, isn't it?

But it never filled, you know,
it just felt heavy
it felt like I was carrying this weight
right here
right here in my blood vessels,
my bloodline
that Mum passed onto me
and her mum passed onto her.

Inherited trauma you could say.
A cesspool of a gene pool
I don't know how to forgive her for that.
I don't know if I can.
I want to though
I want to.
I want to.
I want to.

    Beat.

Nothing is clean in this kitchen.
And all this meat, so red, so violent.

    Beat.

Do you remember Mum's flesh?
Always full of something;

Anyu

so ripe with the spit from his mouth,
blossoming red bruises,
and stems of scars,
she decomposed so fast.

I let her.
I knew the stories
I knew about the men
I knew about what Dad was doing
I knew when she got sick
I knew nursing homes were death camps
I knew how hard it would be
I knew she was weak
I knew she was alone
I knew she felt herself rotting.
And I did nothing
I never helped clean up.
I never did.

I knew how her body was a place of drought
because for years she let him drink her saliva,
her blood
and her tears,
so nothing could grow
and so nothing could fill.
Nothing could avoid the hunger that grew within her.
And I knew that.
And I did nothing.

    Beat.

I remember how she used to cry
with the shower turned up so loud
so we couldn't hear.
But I did.
I always did.
And I would cry along with her

in my bed
hoping that in the morning
she would find my pillow wet
and not feel so fucking lonely.

   Beat.

She left us so quickly
like she didn't want to stay.
She didn't want to stay.
I needed her to stay.
I needed.
I need to clean these dishes
get the dirt off
get it off.
You should be helping, Elliott.

   Beat.

Why was the milk always so sour?

   After frantic scrubbing, IRÉN suddenly halts and more gentle circular motions follow.

   Beat.

finding her like that,
on the clean, white, spotless tiles,
her body so calm,
so quiet.
For the first time,
I only saw soft skin flakes,
I only saw her.

   Beat.

She was my mum.

   Beat.

Anyu

It felt like she melted into
those pale kitchen tiles, melted
somewhere divine, somewhere faraway.

A place you could only reach via a long-distance call.

A place of no harm,
clean bills of health.
Virágzó testek.
Resting heart rates
warm skin.
Csendes szívdobbanások.
A place of tender words
fingers resting on open palms
a place of good mornings
glasses of sweet milk.
Fahéj illatok.
Bacon rashers.
And closeness.

    Beat.

I won't leave till these plates are clean
I won't.
Nem hagyom.

    Beat.

I think Mum and I had the same hands.

    She puts a now clean, spotless plate on the table.

▼ ▼ ▼ ▼ ▼

SOAP
AVA KARUSO

ALICE stands in a bath towel, hair wet, examining a bar of soap. She drops it suddenly in fear. She calls for her dog.

Dip!

> *She looks up to find her sister staring at her.*

Oh. Sisi.
You're here.

No, make yourself at home. That's fine. Whatever.

> *Silence.*

I'm not going with you. I have a date. I know you don't have much time so don't waste it trying to convince me. I've got to be ready when he comes. Have you seen Dip? I think she's chasing the walls again. I don't want her to get lost. Dip! Come here, girl!

Um… no, you're wrong.
And I can leave whenever I want, so shut up.

Sorry.

> *ALICE starts brushing her hair.*

Can you smell that jasmine? I know it died ages ago but I can still smell it. In summer, when all the wood swells up and I feel like this house is going to burst, it's on the air here. Sometimes I can hear the creaky roof beam, too. And that weird bump we never figured out what was. 'It's the ghhhooooost of the aaaaaaattic coooooming to geeeeeet yooooouuuu.'

> *She laughs then stops.*

Soap

Oh, lighten up.
Mum came too, you know. Wanted me to go with her too, and I didn't. Obviously.

You look crap, by the way. You used to be really pretty.

Sorry.

>*Silence.*

It's lovely having this bathroom all to myself. No-one tapping on the door. 'I'll be late to class!' 'Stop wasting water!' 'I need to pee!'

Dip! Where are you?!
I gotta keep her near me or I'm scared she'll get lost.

>*Silence.*

I'm not stupid. I know it's not real.
Doesn't mean he's not coming.
And you know what?
I reckon we might kiss. Like, first kiss! Don't tell anyone I said that. If you tell anyone I said that I will kill you. But that's kinda my mission for tonight. So I gotta look hot. I think he might be the one.

>*ALICE giggles. She sorts through her clothes; they're all dusty and moth-eaten but she doesn't seem to notice. She chooses an outfit and begins to get dressed, making sure her sister doesn't see any of her bits.*

They took down our swing, you know. You weren't here so you wouldn't know but they took it down. They cut the whole tree down. Just killed it 'cause it was in the way of a sewerage line or something. Happened after you left. Mum was here. I didn't think she'd ever leave.

Does this dress look hot or do I look like a prostitute?

Could you just shut up, Sisi?

He is so coming, you liar. Why would you even say that?

Oh, Dip! There you are. No, don't come near me now, you'll get hair all over my dress. Stay. Good girl. You remember Dip, don't you, Sis? Dip's *my* dog now. *Only* my dog. Aren't you, girl? No, no, no, no, no. Stay. Good girl. Doesn't answer to anyone else anymore and she'll do what I say so you'd better watch out.

> Pause.

No, she still remembers you. I was just being mean. I'm sorry. Look, she's wagging her tail.

She still chases the mice in the walls. Remember them? You can smell them in there, can't you, Dip? There's more of them now. Every time Mum put out a trap there were more. Running through the walls, gnawing, rustling, clawing at each other's backs.

Dip's barking at them. I remember that. He's on his way, Sisi, he's coming.

I can hear you shouting and knocking at the door and I know I have to hurry. What if he's here early? And I speed-clean my hair and I'm lathering the soap up all over my arms and I turn around and I see myself, but not in the mirror. There's my doppelganger staring at me, holding a bar of soap, all white and grim and naked. Water running off my shoulders and off its shoulders, our hair thick with bubbles. It's disgusting. And I remember thinking, 'Shit, do I really look like that?' And I know what's going to happen. This harbinger is here for me. And I drop the soap. And I step back—

> ALICE *touches the back of her head and her hand comes back wet with blood.*

I hang in the air above the shower. He arrives to the ambulance sirens, and Mum sends him home. I try to tell you all I'm here but you won't stop crying. Dip barks at me. I know he'll come back for me. When the noise dies down. He'll come kiss me.

Soap

I sink into the walls.
I become part of the building, I become splinters of wood and the leather on the lounge and the air in the fridge.
You get rid of the shower.
And you take down all the photos of me.
And I feel the wind blowing through me.
And you stop crying.
And you leave me.
And I cuddle with Dip every night after Mum buries her.
And I wait at the window.
And Mum stops watering the garden.
And I watch as jasmine flowers wither in your world and blossom in mine.
And you put Mum in a home.
And they take the house.
And I try to gather all the roots I can in my hands but it's not enough.
They cut down all the trees.
And I flee to the attic, but it's all been torn up and there's no roof anymore.
And they pour in cement.
And turn our home into an apartment block—but no-one stays long.
Then into a parking lot where all the cars crash.
Then into a shopping centre.
And Dip and I spend our time smashing plates in shops because our home is gone but there's nowhere else to haunt.

   Silence.

I'm not going with you. I have a date and I think he's the one. Your time's almost up anyway.
I'm sorry you're here, but at least you got to get married, and have kids and get wrinkly and ugly.

I'll go when he comes. I don't care how long it takes. I don't care if he's ugly like you are. I know he's coming. Then we'll go, won't we, Dip?

Should I wear heels or no?

I won't be stuck. I'm waiting. He's coming. He hasn't forgotten me. He never forgot. He wouldn't do that to me. He's the one. He's just taking a while. But I've got Dip to keep me company, don't I, girl? She'll stay because I tell her to.

    Pause.

There you go. It's starting now. It starts at the fingers, they're the first to dissolve.

No. Dip's happy here. That's not fair.

I'm sick of your crap, Sisi. You're lying. I can go whenever I like. I don't need you.

Come here, Dip. Come to me.

I'm staying here with Dip. I'm going on a date. We'll kiss. We'll get drunk in a park and tell Mum we're just tired.

Dip, stay away from her.

Dip.

    Pause.

Please stay.

She's mine.

She's my dog.

You can't take her. This is her home.

Dip, stay.

Dip! You wanna stay too, don't you, girl? Don't you?

Dip?

I won't be—

Soap

Where are you going?

Where—what's going to happen? Tell me what happens?

Trapped?

He'll come get me.

Dip?

Don't take her. Please.

Don't go.

Stay, girl.

You don't understand. I need to be ready.

Dip?

I can move on. I can.

I can.

Just not now.

Please don't go, Sisi.

Dip?

I can.

    Pause.

Can't I?

▼ ▼ ▼ ▼ ▼

PENNY DROPS
BIANCA KOSTIC-LONDON

LIV, a seventeen-year-old Year Twelve student.

Penny drops. Vision blurred, stomach in knots.
Run to the drawer, pull it open, rummage through, there it is.
My purse. It's empty. A post-it note left instead.
You lapsed.
I'm tense; every muscle in my body is tightly wound. Crying with no sound. Stomach punched. Lips quivering, snot falling, tears rain, still no sound.
You win. Free, roaming in opium heaven. You win.
I lose. Trapped, in reality.
Shit, I can't even make a crying sound.
Her room.
Guilt and remorse linger in the air.
> There she is on the lounge. Sound asleep. I wonder how long she has been rested in that position. It's better than the foetal position I noticed she was in as I scurried to school this morning.

I'll pack her bags.
Late for my study session. If I don't pass this fucking bio exam I will fail fail fail.
Grab her some clothes from the laundry.
I've packed your bag. I'm going to Elliot's. I have an exam.
They'll pick you up at nine a.m.
I'd sleep here but I can't, okay.
Find her favourite scarf it smells of Red Door. I'm taken back to the mum I used to know.
Taking one last inhale,
wrap it around my neck,
swallow my tears and paint my positive armour.
Last goodbye.

Penny Drops

  Don't cry, Liv. Don't cry. Hug me, hold me. Tell *me* it's possible to be free.
Love you. Bye.
  Displaced and forgotten and nevertheless between you and I there is a dandelion growing.
The library.
Phone won't stop vibrating in my pocket.
Elliot's called ten times. Can't bring myself to call him back.
Study, study, study.
I've read about polypeptides ten times, nothing sinks into my cloudy brain.
Staring at the images is the closest I get to studying and the furthest I get to achieving my goal of uni.
This is a joke. Joke joke joke.
Phone rings, I answer.
Hey Elliot… sorry I missed your calls, had my phone…
  Autumn leaves can't fall when you are around.
  They're suffocated—thickened—blinded—by your eyes.
  Beneath the stem of each leaf, lies a backbone,
  So slightly bent the moment you acknowledge my existence.
… Can't this weekend… have to study… Gotta go, my phone's flat…
Heater turns off in the library. Tighten scarf. Pack up books.
Air is crisp.
Sit on concrete steps. Stare into night.
Back home.
Oven is off, no smell of cooked spices. I'm hungry.
I water the chillies I planted the weekend Mum left.
Inside their ruby-red cases lie explosions of excitement.
Maybe I will make a chilli jam and give it as a gift to Elliot,
I know he loves hot things. He's impulsive, rebellious and exciting.
Liv making chilli jam *is* weird. You loser!
What eighteen-year-old guy is going to find a girl that hot and

sexy? He can't drip that all over your body and lick it off. Oh, that's just revolting.
Cars zoom by and I realise I have been standing staring at *chillies*. The branches of the bush look like veins that trail off in different directions but they're all attached to the one base.
Didn't go to school. One day won't matter.
Mum's voice hums in the hallway.
Stomach in knots. Muscles clench. The note: Dear…
No.
Get out of house.
The interchange.
Girls talk about formal dresses and shoes; in this moment there is all this talk and it becomes muffled. I'm invisible.
I like it.
I'm normal here. On the outside.
I look at the trees, the vein-like branches hypnotise me. I'll branch out, one day.
The bus blares. I notice someone has drawn a heart on the back window of the bus.
Elliot is at the bus interchange, of course with his charm and Champion Ruby tobacco.
He and I lock eyes and he peels off from his friends towards me. Me, me, me.
Me?! Fine, yeah, fine, good. Always. Today? Today… had a dentist appointment. I wouldn't go that far… My hair… *My hair…* Yeah it's longer I think? A smoke?! Um…

      Be impulsive, Liv. Come off it. He's just your friend.
Yeah. Could you roll me one though? Gabe's party, maybe, not sure.
Reaches out to pass me the ciggie, places it in my hand and tightens his hand over mine.
My muscles unravel as I'm transported for a millisecond into heaven.
Stay here.
Slowly my heaving heart looks up briefly. Stay here.
He catches my aching eyes. Stay here.
You're… lovely.

Penny Drops

I pull away.
Saturdays.
Coffees, magazines, sports and cleaning. Not awaiting your mum too from Warranilla Rehabilitation Clinic.
But that's life, right? No no no no.
My Saturday.
Mum's coming home. Make her bed. Bake a cake.
Lips quiver, vision blurred. Penny drops… Dear…
Don't come in back. I changed the locks. I hate you. I know what you did. I found your sorry note.
You stole from me.
My youth, my money, my hope, my love.
You're gutless.
I hate you I hate you I hate you.
> Dear Baby,
> If you are reading this then you know I have failed. But I couldn't help it… It kills me to do this again. I know I need to go back and get help. This is the last time, I swear.
> I love you.
> Mum.

The door swings open and the sunlight beams behind her.
There it is.
My wild rose.
Hollow, thin.
I yank her towards me.

▼ ▼ ▼ ▼ ▼

THE CLIFFS OF MOHR
KATE McDOWELL

CHRISTINA, an eighteen-year-old girl in her gap year, travelling alone in Ireland. She is a risk-taker, but unsure of her changing identity.

She is sitting in a booth in a bar in a small village pub. Opposite is a middle-aged Irish man. They are each drinking a pint of beer.

[*Sceptical*] I'd love to go but…
This is very weird.

I nearly didn't come out tonight.
There wasn't anyone in my room and…
I've been to pubs on my own before, one in Belfast, but…
It's nerve-racking.
It was really hard to get up and walk out of the hostel, and actually sit down and order a drink.
That sounds stupid, doesn't it?

Even after I walked in, I thought I'd do a lap and if no-one spoke to me, I'd turn around and walk out again.
I've done that a couple of times.

[*Disbelieving*] You said before… I had an aura. Come off it.

You're looking at me intently!

Why do you want to take me?

Won't… Julia?
Be wondering what happened to you?

I can't believe I only met you an hour ago.
[*Laughing*] It was only an hour ago that you stole one of my chips!

Cliffs of Mohr

And now I'm actually thinking about driving with you, up the cliffs of Mohr!

I read about them today. It said they're the most spectacular in Ireland… supposed to be breathtaking.

   She touches her cropped hair.

[*Genuinely inquisitive*] Did you mean it when you said you like my hair?
I think I hate it.

I'm really glad I came out tonight.
I had to get over myself and come out of the hostel.
I spent an hour and a half before I came out here staring at myself in the mirror.

I've been trying to convince myself that it's… pixie. Like I wanted it. And that it actually looks good on me.
I dunno if I believe it.
I was telling myself I look like the kind of girl who cuts her hair short.

I don't even recognise who I'm looking at.

I was becoming obsessive.

I was nearly crying.

And then *you* walk up and spot me.
I just don't understand it.

I was just at the bar, slowly eating my chips.
I wasn't even hungry, I just bought them to have something to do.

And just so you know, I could actually see you in my peripheral vision. I didn't understand why… but I could see you watching me.
So I was actually less surprised when you leaned over my shoulder, and took a chip.

I should have told you off!
But I thought it was great. You could be so cheeky, and get away with it!

You have a very mischievous smile.

I turned around and you were standing there, looking daggy, and grinning like a little kid, munching away and saying you shouldn't have done it.

   She laughs.

And I believe you!

I actually thought then that you don't usually steal people's chips…
How weird.
And egotistical.
But you're not the type, are you?
[*Tongue in cheek*] Nice pants by the way.

The way you were looking at me, it was like… you knew something about me.

I thought… he really wants to speak to me. But everything else was telling me I looked so unlike me, and so invisible, it made no sense.

Well, I thought I stood out, alone on the bar with a haircut that felt fake… but at the same time invisible.
I felt really plain.
And I was still nervous.

I didn't think you were a stalker.
More like a seagull.

That doesn't sound much better, does it?

I *am* a young girl.
And you get told over and over again, how *all* men are.
You know what I mean.

Cliffs of Mohr

And if they're older...

But I don't think you want anything like *that* with me.
I don't think that at all.

I can tell that you don't.

Even if Julia isn't the 'love of your life', I can see how much she means to you.

She sounds like an amazing woman!

So how far is it?
And how many pints have you had?
I don't even know what the legal limit is here.
Are you sure you'd be okay to drive?

I'm going up in the morning, it's okay, you go home to Julia.

My mum called me today. She's crazy. She wanted to know if I'd seen the latest news from home. I have no idea what's happening at home. She rang to tell me all about a German backpacker, who's just been found, well her body was found, in some bushes in the middle of town. Probably less than a k from my house!
She was raped and dumped there.
But she was in Australia with her boyfriend, and then she just went missing.
She was found a few days later.
She wasn't even travelling on her own... but it's creepy that it was in my tiny little town.
It's called Lismore. *You* have a Lismore... I think it's further south, and inland.
I want to go there.

Mum wanted to remind me to be especially careful, blah blah blah.

It's because she cares so much, I know... but she'll give herself a heart attack, and she drives me nuts!

I'll be home in three weeks so I think now she's more nervous than ever that something will happen to me when she's so close to having me back.

I do want to see the cliffs…
And tomorrow… they'll be beautiful, but then… the cliffs in Scotland were beautiful too.
And this is *your* country…
And you're so excited to go…
To show *me*.

   She finishes the end of her beer and plays with her pint glass.

It's amazing thinking about how I thought a year ago.
I remember I thought about people who just roam, alone, without fear, with no set destination.
There was a man in my head, doing this, but he was… it sounds stupid when I say it out loud.
An… ethereal… gypsy spirit.
All brown, with a brown backpack.
Not human, not connected to my world.
He was a hero, for being in control of his own body.
He wasn't restricted by that physical gut fear that holds us back, holds me back, because of humiliation, or whatever.

And now… that god-like creature doesn't exist anymore.
I can just remember how vivid he used to be.

Does this sound crazy to you?

Because here I am, doing this, and… I'm nothing like him.
I'm just me with short hair and a backpack.
But it makes me feel so alive…

Do you want another beer?

[*Surprised*] You *really* want to go now?

   She laughs.

Cliffs of Mohr

She looks about the pub for an excuse to not go, but without finding one…

She picks up her bag.

[*Decisively*] Alright let's go.

▼ ▼ ▼ ▼ ▼

A LANGUAGE OF OUR OWN

BY FAITH NG

The living room. A foldable brown table with two plastic red chairs, one at each end of the table. There's a golden tin of biscuits in the centre of the table. A young Chinese GIRL is sitting at the top end of the table (facing the audience). There's a plate with a biscuit and a can of Coke in front her.

I was at the cemetery with Alvin today, to visit his grandma, his *ah ma*, and tidy up her grave. They had been very close. She took care of him while his parents were at work, even changing his diapers for him. Every afternoon, she would buy him a can of Coke and a packet of *seng bui*. Am I saying it right? *Seng bui*. You know, preserved sour plums?

I guess it doesn't matter; it's not like you understand me anyway. I only speak English and you only speak Teochew, which Dad didn't want to teach me because he said it's a fading dialect from China, so it wasn't a practical language to learn. But I guess it's okay, *Ah Ma*. We have a language of our own, don't you think?

You'll offer me a can of Coke and a large square biscuit. This is your way of saying, 'How are you? I love you.' I'm not hungry, but I'll take it anyway. If I finish it, you'll offer me another one. I'll always finish whatever you give me, no matter how full I am. This is my way of saying, 'I am fine. I love you too.' We'll sit together and I'll eat and you'll watch me eat, and we'll just smile kindly at each other. You'll forget that I've eaten. Every few minutes you'll ask me, '*Jia ba bui?*', which I think means, 'Have you eaten?' And I'll say, '*Jia*', which I think means 'Yes I have'.

Mum said that when she was growing up, biscuits and soft drinks were so expensive. She still remembers the times when she would walk past a bakery and see stacks upon stacks of biscuits neatly packed in gleaming golden tins. She could never afford any of them. She would walk home with an empty stomach.

A Language of Our Own

Is that why you save biscuit tins? I know you keep them as piggy banks. There have been occasions when you've opened a tin, wanting to give me a biscuit, and pulled out money instead. I'll grin at you, willing you to give me the money, but you'll grin sheepishly at me and put it back inside.

Why don't you put your money in the bank? Dad said he tried to convince you to put your money in the bank, but you don't trust them. They take all your hard-earned cash and give you a plastic card. If you're travelling and you get stranded in a foreign land, you can't use the card if you lose it or break it. But, *Ah Ma*, you and I both know you can't travel anymore. You can barely walk, let alone get stranded.

Are you doing this because it connects you to *Ah Gong*? I remember visiting you after *Ah Gong*'s funeral. The house suddenly seemed too big and empty, or maybe you had grown smaller. Dad tried to mask his grief by busily tidying up the house. He was so astonished when he found biscuit tins hidden under the bed, with rolls and rolls of money inside. *Ah Gong* had left his life savings to you by stowing them away in food containers. Dad didn't know whether to laugh or to cry. *Ah Gong* never trusted the government. They made biscuits and soft drinks expensive, and now these are the cheapest things around. He was convinced a conspiracy was going on.

I like your biscuits, even though I could get them anywhere in Singapore. My other grandma never feeds me. She has never fed Mum either. She grew up believing that boys are better than girls. Only a boy can pass the surname of the family down generations.

She only feeds her sons and grandsons. She loves to cook them *sip juan*, this herbal tonic with white noodles and duck meat? She'll make bowls of it for the boys, and when all that's left is the bones and skin of the duck swimming in the brown liquid, fat coagulating at the top, she'll sell it to Mum for fifty dollars—she won't cook for her girls, but she'll sell her food to them. Mum always buys it, even though it's ridiculously overpriced, because she truly believes in how beneficial it is for us, her three daughters.

Recently, Mum started learning how to cook *sip juan*. Her last attempt tasted absolutely like vomit, but we held our noses and drank it anyway and praised her for being a good mother.

Like Mum, I can't cook to save my life. Last winter, I had a huge fight with Alvin when we were studying together in the UK. He stormed out of the house and I sat on the couch in the living room, suddenly frightened by how big and empty the house was. I was so cold and hungry. There was fresh food in the kitchen, but I had no idea how to cook it. I sat there and wondered if this was it, if I was going to starve to death. Snow fell all around me. All of a sudden, I heard footsteps and then the main door burst open and it was him. He slammed the door shut, marched into the kitchen, cooked up a storm, placed it on the table before me and then wordlessly left the house. I ate and my heart swelled with love and warmth.

At his grandma's grave this morning, I watched him lay out two small red cups of tea, a can of Coke, a packet of *seng bui*, a few packs of cigarettes, and he said to her, '*Ah Ma, jia, jia*'. Eat, eat. And then he smiled at her black-and-white photo, and she simply smiled into the distance beyond him.

You're right here before me, *Ah Ma*, but I feel like I've already lost you. All I have are glimpses and guesses and snatches of stories.

I want to talk to you, ask you how your day is like, what you think about, how you became something from nothing, what you think about me, the girl who stands on the shoulders of generations of women like you but speaks English, the language of foreigners, and gets a boy to cook for her, if you miss home, if you miss your parents, if you miss *Ah Gong*, if you're happy, if there's anything I can do to thank you for the life you've made possible for Dad, and hence, for me.

I've tried to bridge the gap between us. I've tried to pick up Teochew. But the language is so complex that my tongue is unable to bend and twist its way into pronouncing those words. It's easier to put a piece of biscuit into my fat and flat tongue and chew and smile at you as you smile at me and watch me eat.

▼ ▼ ▼ ▼ ▼

THE PANEL

LAUREN SHERRITT

TIM walks on stage. He has put in effort, slicked-back hair, ironed shirt, clean teeth. He feels he is in for a win. He squints through the lights into the audience. A big breath.

Wow! Look at you all! St Francis, the original; Marie Curie, the science nerd, Saddam Hussein—keeping it controversial! All of you here! Jesus up the back there! What a beard, man! Gandhi's still off with one of the angels, hey? Saucy saucy! How's that Arc, Joanie? Ha *ha!* Ha. God, wow—Can I just start off by saying, and I know it's probably not *my* place to start off, that it is *such* an honour to be here with you today. Just such a—
What?
Oh, of course. Timothy Young. I just think that—
December sixteen 2011. I'd been working pretty intensely for a couple of weeks there, but yes, December sixteen was the day. The old beast just walked right up behind me and *pow!* So how does this work? You just ask me questions or—?

A question is asked.

Oh! Okay. Well, there's a tough one right off the bat! Why I want to be a martyr…
Well, to be honest I feel it's the place I rightly deserve to be. I've been stuck out there with all the, you know, more pedestrian types, and I just don't fit in. I mean it's hardly like I just had your average life/death journey, is it? When it happened, the death, I was a little bit woozy. I didn't really realise what was going on, and by the time I came to, well, decisions had been made. I'm sure it's just a clerical error; things must get pretty busy up here this time of year. But yeah, I mean, pretty esteemed company and all, but I belong up here with you guys.

Question.

Alrighty. Well, it was Mr Bryans, the science teacher, who first told me about the cows. It just made me feel sick. You know my dad's had sun cancer before, right on his nose? Caused by that great big hole in the ozone layer. And that, Mr Bryans said, was caused by cows. Can you believe it? Cows. Little old Daisy out the back chewing on her grass and farting up a big old cloud of sunny death. Got me thinking, didn't it?

Question.

Well, sure it's a big issue. Seas are rising, man, and things are changing. When I was a kid, to give you an example, an ice-cream cone would last you for-ever. Forever! Now it's 'walk outside and the whole thing's melted in your lap'. It's going to wipe out all those Melapenasian types first with the water, but we'll all go one way or another. Cultures lost. Sad stuff. Sad stuff.

Question.

Well, that's my one regret, for sure. That my work isn't finished. That ozone layer's still one big holey Earth cardigan and I'm up here feeling pretty useless. Which is why the martyrdom thing would really help me out.

Question.

Well, at the moment, no-one's really seeing my work for what it was, what it could be, but a little boost in the PR situation and I feel like the world could really be changed. It's all about appearance. You get that, don't you, Joanie? I don't know if they'd have gone 'death at stake' if you hadn't been so extreme on the 'I want to wear pants and fight like the boys' line. But you don't get to be a martyr being one of the popular kids, do you now? Hazard of the job!

Beat.

Look, it's a dirty job, but it needs doing and obviously it can't be me anymore. I just feel like if my face starts appearing on

The Panel

people's toast, maybe it'll help with the inspiration.

Question.

How did I do it? It's really simple, like a kind of plug? Or maybe more like a wine cork, yeah, on a fancy bottle.

Question.

Well, I've got one up here if you'd like to see, I could just run and—

Question.

Usually brown. No need to get too fancy. Round obviously. Round plug, round hole works best. The materials were hard to get right, and I'd still be open to suggestion actually, but—

Question.

No. No, I do need to be honest and say it wasn't my own idea to start with. Will that count against me? It was actually my mate Marty, from school, he came up with it to start off with, can't believe he actually just gave away such a winning idea, but he was never one to get off his arse and actually do anything.
The boys didn't think I'd go through with it, you know, they didn't think I'd have it in me. They laughed and laughed when they told me, and I heard one of them, Johnno, whisper to Marty, 'Aw, man, he'll never do it!' Well, didn't I just prove them wrong, hey?

Question.

Dangerous? Too damn right it was dangerous! We're talking cows, here, bovines! They might look like it from up here, but they're not that small! Up to here on me some of them would come, higher if they were a bit angry or on a hill!

Question.

Yeah, there's opposers all over the place! Apart from the

farmers who were all sorts of jumpy, those goddamn Christian lobby groups— pardons, Jesus— but can you talk about a bunch of head-in-the-sands?! And don't make me start on the pollies, don't make me start!
Oh. Sure. I can see your point. It was all a bit more primitive when most of you were around, sure. These days it's all talk, talk, talk, not as much physical danger—
No, no! No, I only mean that... I'm certainly not calling you... Well, you still wear the sandals, but—
Well, hang on a minute there—

A statement.

'Not martyr material'. Wha— ?!

Statement.

No, hang on, you can't just leave! What do you mean 'not quite the right story'? What kind of story do you want? 'Man plugs cows, saves world!' If you look at it again I think you'll see it's beautiful in its simplicity!

Statement.

Well, how are we going to save the world then? No offence to anyone here, but you've had a while, and I'm pretty sure some advanced warning, and none of you guys have managed to make any kind of difference. You've got fucking Madame Curie over here, Madame 'I radiationed myself to death but *I* still got to be counted as a martyr', and you've failed to see what I, a simple guy with a simple life, has managed to not only recognise but find a solution for.

Statement.

Well, it's no crucifixion, sure, but it fucking hurt. A plug of that size backfiring at such a speed puts a hole clean through a man!

Statement.

You can't be serious. I don't belong out there. I am a martyr!

The Panel

Look, I don't want seventy-one virgins, or to sit just to the left of God or to eternally eat cheese or swim in chocolate lakes or anything. I just want it to be recognised that I was a good guy, doing a good thing, and I died because of it. Those are the terms and conditions for martyrdom, right?

    Statement.

No, I certainly do not put myself above— No, no, I'm a man of the people! But, those people, they died for nothing. Old age or cigarettes or breaking speed limits or not refrigerating the prawns properly.
I died for something. Just like you. Just like you! Right?

    Statement.

Well…I—I just can't believe it.
Too dirty for you, am I? Not 'pure' enough. Actually got my hands in and did the work! Look, I've read those reports on Gandhi and the sex stuff, oh boy, have I read! You're not all as pure and holy as you think you are!
Security? Really?! You're calling security?! Not prepared to fight your own fights, hey? Hey?! Well, that's just typical, isn't it, get your little posse to come and win your battles. Where are you going? How dare you— ?! *I shoved plugs up cows for this—!*

    A sudden lightning bolt, thunder crashes. TIM drops to the floor.

▼ ▼ ▼ ▼ ▼

OLD KING COAL
FREGMONTO STOKES

It is night-time. There is a tall wire fence, grass stretching out behind it into darkness. A railway line can just be made out in the distance. REBECCA MIDWAY, aged seventeen, stands in front of the fence, a large bag in one hand and a saw in the other. As she talks, she begins sawing at the bases of the fence poles, of which there are three visible.

On this day one year ago I stood on this earth before this fence and looked out across that stretch of grass at that rail line. Coal trains run along that line all the way to Newcastle. There were four hundred of us here, the makeshift marching band blaring, clowns honking their noses, grim reapers waving scythes, radical cheerleaders shaking pompoms, and Christians asking, 'What would Jesus do?'
The fence fell and we walked over it before the police could rein us in. We sat down on the rails and stayed there the whole day.
Wennie the tuba player was arrested first, she was dwarfed by both her instrument and the officers. An eighty-seven-year-old man, wilting in the sun, was taken away next. The rain started falling, the police closed in, and we started dancing. First the Nutbush, then the Bus Stop—by the time we got to the Chicken Dance the police had surrounded me.

She chicken dances as she recalls the conversation.

Name please?
Rebecca Midway.
Are you aware if you do not leave immediately you can be arrested for trespassing?
Yes.
Do you wish to leave?
No.

She stops chicken dancing.

Muswellbrook [*pronounced 'Muscle-brook'*] police station wasn't big enough to hold everyone, so in the end fifty people got arrested, and we got an article on page eight of the *Sydney Morning Herald*. We felt the protest had been a success, but as it turned out they couldn't have cared less. We could call them fat cats, running dog and corporate vultures and summon up every other animal from the mythical bestiary of the impotent, but for what end?

Pause. As REBECCA speaks, she starts rummaging through her bag.

Before the protest last year I stayed up till dawn, wondering whether I would get arrested or not. I stayed up till dawn last night too, wondering whether I should lay this bomb on the rails or not.

She pulls a bomb and assorted wires out of the bag, imitating the host on a cooking show.

Yes, tonight I'll be tying a bomb to those railway tracks. It will be a strictly non-violent bomb, in the sense that I'm not planning to kill anyone, except perhaps myself through lack of familiarity with explosive devices.

Now I know bombs aren't such a marketable green product, it doesn't resonate with our target demographic; it's a hard sell to a doctor's wife on the North Shore or in Toorak:

She pretends to be on the phone talking to a doctor's wife, putting on her best, charming, call centre voice.

'Oh hello, Valerie is it? Yes well, Valerie, this month at Greenwash Inc. we've got a fabulous range of green campaigns that you can sponsor, we've got some delicious fair trade Incan tapioca and mung bean friands that you can order online, and a lovely eco-micro-financing scheme in Africa… Yes that's right, just like on the TV… Yes Africa is a very sad country, isn't it?… But it's people like you who care who make the difference… Oh great, yes we can do that by credit card; look Valerie, we've also got a little bomb attack planned for the

Hunter Valley rail line that you can add on as a sort of bonus with the friands— Hello Valerie?'

She stops the imaginary call, briefly disappointed, then addresses the audience.

I don't know, what do you think would make bombs more marketable, say, to the youth demographic? How would you feel if I said that I'd got the gelignite as an added extra in a zine swap, that it was a little D.I.Y. bomb with a quirky 'lolcat'-ism written on the front: 'I iz on ur railway line disrupting the smooth flow of capital, woot'. Perhaps if I'd found the gunpowder while fossicking for some cute kitschy vintage dresses in a country op-shop, would that make it acceptable? It's kind of hard for bombs to have the same ironic charm as blaxploitation films or badge making.

But surely there's another option— surely a bomb attack is a bit extreme. Would you recommend a Facebook campaign instead: 'Unlike coal, lol'?

Then again, you could rig up a corpse to a computer, and if it was in the first twitchy stages of rigor mortis it could click the mouse just as well as a living human. Sorry, I'm just a bit sceptical about any form of activism that can be done by a cadaver. Look, I've got nothing against us trying a few more peaceful mass protests either. But a bomb could stop the coal trains running for a fortnight instead of a day, and if it can do more without anyone being hurt, what's the big deal?

I wonder how history will judge my little bomb and I, if by chance I fumble and blow myself up tonight.

Having sawed almost all the way through the last pole, she pushes the fence and it collapses.

Well, it's time.

Don't feel like you need to come with me, you're free to stay where you are. They'll probably put the fence back up again, same as they did last time. But if you start to notice water lapping at your heels, and you feel like moving, I'll leave the saw here for you.

Old King Coal

She walks over the fence, without looking back, and disappears into the darkness.

▼ ▼ ▼ ▼ ▼

A LIVING ROOM
JESSICA TOVEY

A living room. There is a sign hanging on the wall: 'You'll be missed'. HEATHER is setting up for a party. There's champagne, a cake, party hats and a range of nibbles laid out. She speaks on her mobile phone hands-free.

Tell them I'll only do it if I get to dance with… the teethy one? Marcus or Marco— Todd's clearly sleeping with him and always gives his routines nines and tens. And no sequined midriffs, I've shown enough skin for one lifetime and I'm trying to be taken seriously now.

    She hangs up. She continues setting up for the party.

Where the hell are they?

    Her mobile rings.

Hey, sis, I'll have to leave you hands-free. I'm still setting up.
No, not yet. Mum and Dad are out for dinner, so get ready to party.
A wake?
No, it's a party.
I know what it is.
I know she has.
I guess it is, then.
Well, I've just bought all this champagne, is that appropriate for a wake?
So when are you getting here?
What? Why?
You can't let me drink alone.
No, of course I won't be, the others will be here any sec.

Shit. Time. It's starting, turn your telly on.

A Living Room

I can't watch it by myself.
Watch it with me, just till they get here.
Oh, come on.
Turn it on.
I should TiVo this.
Bound to be a good laugh. Maybe I'll show it at my twenty-first?
Actually, that'd be pretty weird.
Turn it on, please.
I can't go to my own funeral alone.

She switches on the TV with her remote. A theme song can be heard starting up.

Thanks.
It'll be fun.

Pause.

Are those gerberas in my wreath?
You'd think they could fork out for some lilies or something.
Angel would have white lilies.
Or roses, gardenias even, but not…

Bruce came! I didn't know he was coming.
Strange him being here—he and Angel rarely had scenes together.
Love that man. He's such a trooper; one kidney and still with a nose like Rudolf.
I *saw* that article.
Assholes!
Why don't they leave him alone?
Fifteen years in that place would make anyone drink.

Are you kidding?
All those five a.m. starts.
God no, don't regret it.
Jesus, two years was more than enough.

Drinking milkshakes in Marge's cafe was hardly the career goal.
The place was...

What?
Who said?
Who told you that?
Of course it was my decision to leave.
It was my choice! I chose.
Who told you that?
Well, you have to tell me now.
Was it Brent?
It was Brent!
It was, wasn't it?
That shit.

Look at him.
Couldn't act his way out of a paper bag.
D'you see that?
Brent, with the tears.
Bet they used the blowie.
Couldn't even cry at his own wife's funeral.
Told you.
Not. Even. Out of a paper. Bag.
I swear, if he starts hugging my coffin I'm going to hurl.
Bullshit!
Being an inflated steroid junkie doesn't make you an actor.
Yes he does, I should know.
There was this one night.
One, drunken night.
Once!
Charity ball.
Like two tiny grapes, that's how I know.

What's so funny?
You just laughed.

A Living Room

Yeah, you did.
What were you laughing at?
Was it the 'None of our lives will be the same without her' part?

Oh.
Grapes, right.
I know, gross.

Yeah, of course they'll be here soon, they're just a little bit late.

Oh, okay, sure, but be quick, you don't want to miss anything.

Christ, a photomontage? That's a bit much.

This is really weird.

It had its moments though, didn't it, Angel? Remember that one? They took it on our first day, when we came to town and we were nearly mown down by that runaway tractor and Derrick saved us and he like totally fell in love with us right on the spot. God, he was a sweetheart, wasn't he? He's on 'Rush' now, yeah; he's really going places… Oh, the school dance. Angel, we looked so fierce that night. But then we had to give birth in that tree 'cause the stalker, who turned out to be that possessed priest, was hunting us down. Such a waste of an Alex Perry gown… Oh, the helicopter crash out at sea! Man, that night was cold and we're like out shooting till like five in the morning. Those sneaky bastards, making us stay in the ocean the whole time with that stupid, tiny wetsuit on that kept riding up the crack of our ass. Aww, lovely Soph from make-up kept giving us those cups of hot chocolate, but they just got full of seawater and tasted like shit… I kinda loved that night.

Oh, yeah, still here.
No, you didn't miss much.
They're doing a photomontage—cliché.

I like those ones of Luke and I, though.
They're actually, kinda, quite sweet.

That was about the time we first hooked up.

You knew that.
My last three months.
It's not like he's my real brother.
What?! When?
But she's our mother, well not our real mother, but she's old enough.
Oh… that's disgusting. When?
Okay, now I feel sick.

   She watches for a while.

They all look so sad.
Wonder if… [anyone actually is?]
Oh, Julie's crying.
She actually looks like she's really crying.
I miss her.

It's quite… [moving] … good music.

There'd be people crying right now.
Millions, crying.
Their final farewell.
Goodbye, to their dear friend Angel.

What's with the grave? Why are they doing that?
I asked specifically to be cremated.

You're damn right, this is more bloody morbid.
It's…
Why didn't they tell me?
Somebody should have asked me.
Well, what if…?
What about Angel's claustrophobia storyline?!
It's not very true to character.
Well, what if I'm afraid of the dark or… worms?
I know that but they should have… [asked me.]

A Living Room

Oh, Cindy, there you are!
Oh, sis, you're comforting Brent.
You're crying.
For me.
Aww, Cindy, you look so miserable, so sad to see your sister go.

Pause.

Rachel, Rach.
I know.
I meant, Rachel; I'm not stupid.
Jesus, I know.
I know you're not… really Cindy, Rach.
I just meant your character… looked so…

Pause.

Don't worry about it.
I should let you go, I'm sure you have to get up early.
Four a.m.! God, don't miss those. What are you filming?
Who's that?
Oh, a newbie. Who does she play…?

Wow.
Didn't take Brent long to move on.
I guess I should be grateful it's not my mother.

I've got to be up early myself.
Just got some writing to do, I'm working on my own script at the moment.
A film, yeah, it's really great exploring other sides of my creativity. It's meaty too, you know, something to really sink my teeth into.
Sure… yeah… I'd love for you to read it… but it's still really in a draft phase.

Oh, yeah, I meant to say congrats before, on your nomination.
I was nominated for a Logie once; you'll have a blast.
Two?

Best Newcomer and Most Outstanding?

> *Pause.*

Well...

Tell them all I say hi.
Yes.
Yes.
I said yes!

Actually I think I can hear some people arriving now. But we should catch up. Free this weekend.
Oh, yeah, of course you'll...
Well, soon then.
Call me.
Night. Night, Rach.

> *She sits for minute. She slices a piece of cake, pours herself another glass of champagne. She picks up the remote. Hits rewind. Stops. Presses play.*
>
> *The theme song starts up again.*

▼ ▼ ▼ ▼ ▼

LESSON 88
JESSIE TU

A young pregnant GIRL, in a willowy dress, steps onto the stage: tired smile, blushed cheeks. She is holding a banana in her hand. A single stool is at the centre of the stage.
She sits on it, back straight, and smiles to the audience.
She extracts a remote control and clicks it.

Lesson 88.
Okay, old sport.
Let's get this going.

> *Pause, then she takes a breath.*

Come on, don't laugh.
This is *serious*.
It looks silly and funny, but it's very important you listen carefully, because if you don't…
if you don't…!

> *Pause.*

Let's just not go there right now… I've got to go back to the hospital…

> *She holds up the banana.*

so…

> *She takes out a condom and rips it open with her teeth.*

you take the rubber… and roll it out like so…
and then… use two hands now…
and… then…

> *She slips the condom over the banana in one quick action.*

Violà!
See, easy!

> *She extracts her remote again and clicks it again.*

Lesson 23. No television.
I wasted my childhood on that ridiculous invention.
Your dad and I didn't have one when we met, and we didn't have one when we bought our first house. And we don't plan to have one when you are born.
Make sure your dad doesn't start going to your rugby matches, because I know your father and I know what happens on the sidelines of those footie games.
They don't just talk about their sons…
If kids at school start talking about what some mongrels did on 'Big Brother' last night, just listen, and nod. And smile. Act like you think it's funny— because it is… ordinary people watching the ordinary lives of ordinary people.

[*Whispering*] Don't tell your dad I told you this, but he's actually secretly in love with reality television…
[*Loudly*] Your silly dad!

> *Pause.*

I remember visiting his house for the first time…
It was littered with cat-piss pots, and the windows were blindless and painted in bird shit and Nana Anne was smoking on the couch with her pipe hanging loosely at the end of her thickish lips and her eyes looked red and bruised and she stared at me snarly like I was some intruder and your dad…
he…
he…
your dad…
he just stepped right across the dump and leant over and…
and…
he kissed Nana Anne on the cheeks.

> *Beat.*

Lesson 88

I'm sorry. You needn't hear all this... I'm getting carried away. No TV.

> DAD calls from offstage: 'You can watch your shows online anyway!'

Henry! This is *my* message to Jacob, thank you!

> She extracts the remote and clicks it.

Lesson 17.
So... you just got roughed up by some nasty guys?

You know the cleverest men who ever lived on this planet were bullied?

God! I want to be there to *punch them in the face!* Those idiots are just jealous of you. You've got a head they'll never have. *Of course* they'd be mad at you!

> Pause.

Just remember... no-one, ever... *ever*...
from the millions and billions and trillions of people who have ever lived before you has ever been like you...and no-one ever will be.
Don't forget that.

> She extracts the remote and clicks it.

* * * *

Lesson 55. How to ask her out.

> Pause.

So... old sport. You fancy a girl real well, eh?
Now... what to do?

> Pause... she thinks.

Well, go up to her, old sport, coz girls like it when boys step up

and take action.
So… who's this girl? She pretty?
I bet she is.
Make sure she's in the nice girls group. You know… the girls with their skirts covering their knees and ribbons in their hair.
Good, nice, modest girls who won't break your heart.
So… befriend her first. Have a few conversations. Ask her about a maths algorithm… an English assignment.
Then, pick a day… not too cloudy, not too sunny, and say nicely… 'What are you doing this Friday night? There's a great pizza place I know on King Street, do you wanna come?'
See?
Easy.
If she has a boyfriend, pretend he doesn't exist.

>*She extracts the remote and clicks it.*

Lesson 45. How to drive.
Sixteen!
You can drive now!

>*Pause.*

Fuck, life goes fast, eh?

>*Pause.*

Don't try to get behind the wheel of your dad's Jaguar.
Don't even *try*.
Take my old Barina.
It's my little honey bun, but I'd like you to have it.
Make sure your hair is out of your face!
You want to be able to *see* when you're driving…
When I was in high school, it was trendy for boys to have a mop of oily hair that sleeked across their face: like they were trying to be all cool and mysterious.
Totally stupid, I know.
Don't they know that cool is not mysterious and mysterious is not cool?

Lesson 88

Sorry. Mum's getting carried away again.
Start slowly.
Don't grip the wheel too tight.
Oh, and… make sure you're logging all your hours of driving in that glossy book provided by the RTA. Don't cheat like your mum did.
And drive twice as slow at night.

> *She extracts the remote and clicks it.*

* * * *

She has a silk scarf wrapped tightly round her head.
She extracts the remote slowly…

Lesson… oh, what is it now?
I can't remember.
But… you're eighteen years old.

> *Pause.*

You're a man now.

> *Sigh.*

This is my last message to you. You don't need me to teach you anything.

> *Pause.*

You've carried me with you these eighteen years… now… you'll continue without me…
I'm off on another path… that's all it is. Departure.
Sometimes, it's unexpected… and… that's what hurts people. The shock. But… old sport… you always knew this was coming… right?

> *Pause.*

I didn't sleep well last night.
I think I've spent these past few weeks losing sleep over you,

old sport. You're not even in this world yet… and making myself sick over you.

    Pause.

It's so quiet now.
Where is your dad?
Out in the garden?

    Pause.

    She looks down at her belly… sighs deeply, pacing the stage slowly, caressing her belly.

Don't be afraid. See the world! Love, but love sensibly. Find a good wife for your soul [*aside:*] and sanity… [*Also aside:*] Oh, and old age: that *will* come. [*Not aside:*] Find someone who will love your nature and accept your scars.
Don't forget to visit me… once a year is enough.

▼ ▼ ▼ ▼ ▼

www.ingramcontent.com/pod-product-compliance
Lightning Source LLC
Chambersburg PA
CBHW050033090426
42735CB00022B/3473